The Zymoglyphic Anthology

An assemblage
of documents
from and about
the **Zymoglyphic Museum**

INTRODUCTION

The Zymoglyphic Museum, located in Portland, Oregon, is the world's only institution devoted to the study and display of art, artifacts, and culture of the Zymoglyphic region. Its publishing arm, the Zymoglyphic Museum Press, was founded in 2009, tasked with documenting the museum as a printed book, as well as providing a literary dimension to a primarily visual art project, a metaphorical third leg to its physical and cyberspace incarnations.

The museum's press has, in the intervening decade, produced three more books and a wide variety of zines, pamphlets, and exhibition catalogs. The first part of this compendium, "Curator's Corner," gathers a selection of these smaller works together in one handy portable volume, along with archival documents relating to the history of the museum.

Visitors to the museum are sometimes inspired to create their own artistic responses to the museum, its exhibits, and artifacts. The second part of this book, "Orbital Views," showcases some of these responses in a wide variety of media - fiction, photography, essay, and more.

Jim Stewart
Editor
Curator of the Zymoglyphic Museum

Contents

Curator's Corner

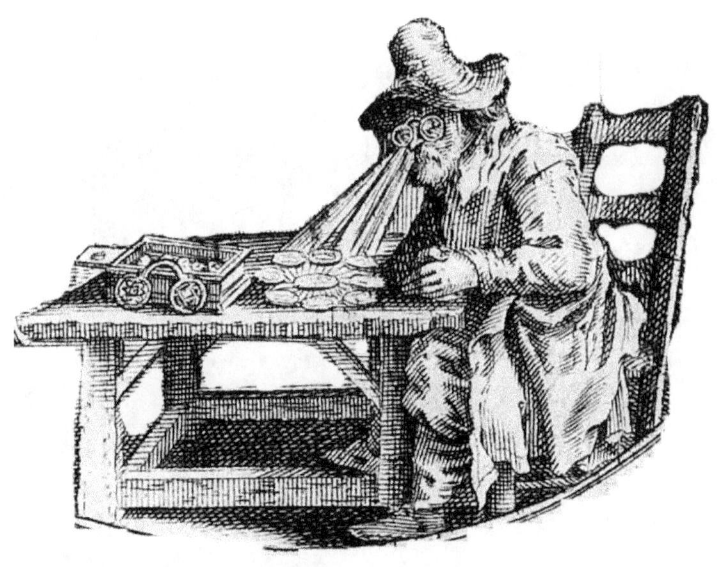

The Zymoglyphic Way

A Manifesto

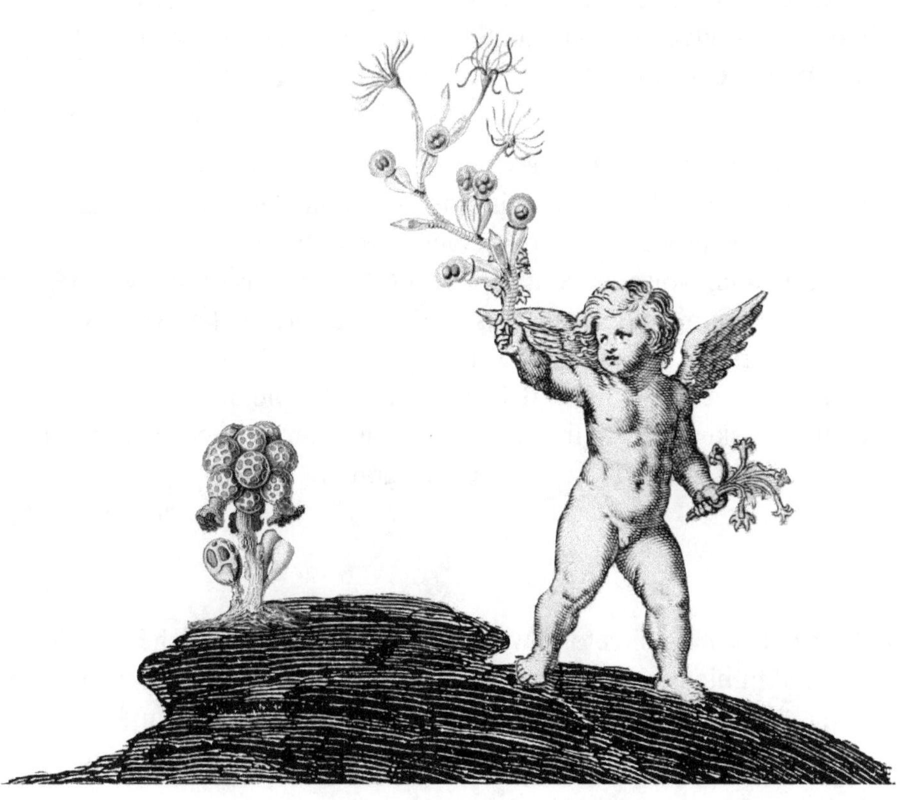

I.

We of the Zymoglyphic region stand in awe of the vastness of the cosmos, the miracle of molecules coming to life, the strangeness of life's evolutionary byways, and the peculiarities of the quantum structure on which it all rests, all described in mathematical and taxonomic detail to us by our astronomers, our biologists, and our physicists.

Even so, we feel dissatisfied with the limitations inherent in the immutable laws of physics and we look to our artists and storytellers to imagine further an enchanted universe populated with chimeras and mythical beings, the flora and fauna of the jungles, deserts, and swamps of our internal continents.

Our principles are not always clear - we have desires for both simplicity and complexity, for lean design and for worlds within worlds, for adventure and domesticity. We value ancient artifacts and fragile ephemera.

We accept that decay is inevitable and we find poetry in it. We believe that the best we can do is slow down the decomposition and examine the process. We counteract entropy with our own acts of creation. Our Museum contains the mortal remains of many beings in a state of arrested decay. Dust and grime bedeck the exhibits and spiders are encouraged to add their embellishments. We accept that the great Museum itself will one day be a picturesque ruin, its columns askew, its engines rusted, its halls run to weeds and vines, its exhibits scattered, crushed, and forgotten.

II.

Some of us are collectors; we collect the marginalia of the world. We find miniature worlds in hidden places and try to bring them home. We see art in gnarled roots, agate slices, and rusty metal. We are fascinated by the things in the world that straddle boundaries:

hybrids and chimeras, the artist who is a scientist, the taxidermied corpse that seems to be alive.

We are also creators. Our goal is to illuminate the correspondences between the wonders of the physical world and the phantasms and spirits of our psyches. Our creations are spontaneous, adventurous, wondrous, and wildly inconsistent yet strangely coherent.

We submit our collections, our simple creations, and our artifacts, as offerings to our great Museum in the hope that the Museum will find proper places for them in the grand cosmography of its august halls, its exhibits, and its research facilities. We turn to the dusty microcosm of our great Museum to help us with understanding and connection. Like the world, our Museum has its hidden rooms and forgotten corners, and little museums within it.

III.

There is poetry in decay and an authenticity in layers of weathering that cannot be duplicated by a deliberate hand

There is meaning in a spontaneous sketch, in a quick assemblage of detritus and gnarled sticks found on the same day or found years apart, as if meeting at long last.

There is discovery to be had in creating without knowing what the final product will be or why it even exists at all.

We embrace the amateurs, the outsiders, the impatient ones, those who create just to create, with no regard for commercial viability or success

We abjure polish and shine and will merely tolerate meticulous craftsmanship; we value dust on our objects and take spiderwebs as compliments.

We are unbowed in our roles as Jacks and Jills of all media, masters of none. We prefer variety to specialization or consistency, understanding that the whole will be greater than the sum of its parts.

The value of a created object comes from its meaning, its creativity, and its ability to inspire creativity in others; not its craft, its precision, its cleanliness, its scarcity, nor the fame of its maker.

IV.

As with the evolution of life from the primordial ooze, let complexity arise out of simplicity by its own accord; begin with nature; collaborate with nature; let nature do the detail work.

Collect and arrange, plunge in and create; if your collected objects have personalities, arrange them into mysterious narratives; explicate the narrative later if at all; step back in space or in time, observe what you have made, and tell stories about what you have made.

Be unconcerned that what you make has been made before; likewise be unconcerned that it may be made again by others; it is your own uniqueness that is the essence that cannot be duplicated. As Qoheleth said millenia ago, "There is nothing new under the sun." If it is meaningful to you, it has value; if it inspires others, it has value.

Curator's Resume

&

Artist's Statement

Curator's Resume

Objective

Integrate diverse elements from a wide variety of media into a conceptually unified syncretic framework, with proven results in both the physical and virtual worlds.

Accomplishments

Establishment of the Zymoglyphic Museum, internationally recognized as the world's foremost authority on the history, ecology, and culture of the Zymoglyphic region, eagerly pursuing excellence as a fictocryptic institution

Creative endeavors in a full range of media from primitive pencil drawing to algorithmically-driven computer animation, including painting, assemblage, collage, writing (both archaic and modern), and digital photography. Minimal skill sets in selected areas are compensated by spontaneity, variety of media, and lack of competition in newly-created genres

Autodidact in Esoteric Museology

Responsibilities

Diorama development, design and construction of museum exhibits, and creation, collection, conservation, and curation of museum artifacts

Editor, publisher, writer, photographer, and book designer for the Zymoglyphic Museum Press

Museum Web site design and maintenance
- User-centered interface design with emphasis on easy navigability
- Design and development of online educational exhibits
- Fitful updating of the museum's official Web log

Results-oriented marketing
* Design and promotion of collateral merchandise for the museum's online shop
* Proven linguistic malfeasance in promoting the Zymoglyphic brand
* Leverages best practices to take the paradigm to the next level, enabling full 360 degree turnaround
* Lackadaisical mismanagement of the museum shop's marketing efforts, resulting in gross sales reaching well into double digits, thereby preserving the museum's non-profit status
* Ineluctably sesquipedalian vocabulary

Administration of museum outreach programs
* Official greeter and tabulator during museum open days
* Sales associate and cashier for museum shop
* Maintain sangfroid in the face of innocent but annoyingly repetitious questions
* Liaison activity with affiliated institutions
* Management of the museum's social media presence

Scholarly research on the Zymoglyphic region; organization, management, and financing of expeditions thereto

Artist's Statement

My work explores the nascent dialectic between naive eccentricity and self-referential parody in the creation of an institutional persona. The "Zymoglyphic Museum" is both a site-specific environmental installation and a transgressive multi-media institution that blurs the boundaries between the display space and the creative process; it operates as a syncretic amalgam filling the interstices of creation and curation.

The paradoxical conjunction of the museum is further compounded by the museum's quotidian architecture and anodyne siting on the one hand, and, on the other, its fermented holdings, its fabled grotesqueries, corrosive stochastic processes, and unbridled entropic transmutations, all enveloped in an overarching serendipitous miasma.

The museum confronts contemporary art's expectation that it provide a cultural critique, perhaps by subverting the role of museums as authoritative institutions, or by questioning its Eurocentric appropriation of Asian cultural paradigms, or at least commenting sardonically on consumer waste and the destruction of the environment; instead, the museum merely indulges in transcendentally whimsical sesquipedalian revelry.

[T]he "artist statement" [is] a contested site of practice, a discursive form where writing meets (or, variously intrudes upon, supplements, contextualizes, contradicts, enhances, extends, or gestures toward) visual arts production and exhibition. In the context of interdisciplinary and multidisciplinary research, the artist statement (which more conventionally introduces, contextualizes, and describes an artist's work for public exhibition) has the potential to become both a vehicle for creative inquiry and an alternative to more traditional means of academic dissemination.

-- W.F. Garrett-Petts and Rachel Nash, "Re-Visioning the Visual: Making Artistic Inquiry Visible" *Rhizomes: Cultural Studies in Emerging Knowledge* 18 (2010). Retrieved 15 Nov 2012

Tour the Museum with Joyce and Re-joyce!

The Zymoglyphic Museum was one day haunted by the spectre of Modernist literature's pre-eminent figure, James Joyce. The resulting quagmire of puns and multi-use words was captured in real time and is presented here as told.

```
A decent young docent named Joyce
Was recently given no choice:
She could not see him
In the museum
But she spoke in her namesake's voice!
```

The transcrypt of the twour

Well, come to the The Zyglomorphic Amusing Rheum! Lots
of Fun with Finnegans Wake!

*Penetrators are permitted into the museomound free. For
her passkey supply to the janitrix, the mistress Kathe. This
is the way to the museyroom. Mind your hats goan in!*

This is a goodly cabinet with a chitinous crabinet, a coleop-
terous mycocosm of myth and mayhap, of dottles and orts,
swirls within whirls within whorls, mortifaction and calcifiction, a composition in compost.

*What a mnice old mness it all mnakes! A middenhide hoard
of objects!*

These are the die-oramas, crude cerebrations of animala-
tions, a mothy paradise for fora and flauna, mummyfied and
deadified, petrified and putrified.

*a weird of wonder tenebrous as that evil thorngarth, a field
of faery blithe as this flowing wild*

This rheum dates from the Late Crustaceous!

These are pulchritudinous picktures from the pickled
passed, left in the dust and *laid to rust upon the green.*

These are the arktifacts that harken back, in fact, to wan-
drous daze, inspiring promordiol "oooh!"s, from an arkeo-
logic and arkapelagic land enfalloped in fog and mistery.

*you would see in his house of thoughtsam...what a jetsam
litterage of convolvuli of time lost or strayed, of lands derelict and of tongues laggin, too.*

Thish is a fish that murmur made, *the crux of the catalogue of our antediluvial zoo*, a psychordelic mating plaice for ye of liddell fate, off to wander land.

Though Wonderlawn's lost us forever. Alis,alas, she broke the glass!

But the winnegan's fake.

See what happens when your somatophage merman takes his fancy to our virgitarian swan?

This swan's Mayan and that wan's urine!

This is the zymic lab'ratory, demoted to the supplimation, redaction, and collusion of allusionogenic substances, alife with deoxyribonucleic gyrations and possum- and proper-bilities.

This is, in some, a grand fissionary tombessence, teaming with troglodytes and zyglomorphs in constint fluxus, a restless peripatesis, eternally seeking the great cerulean circumaximtranssubstantiation!

Transfusiasm!

For is it not inscripchewered: "a dream cometh through the multitude of business..." (and hear we quoteth the sagely Qoheleth)

A zymonesiac emission from the post-orifice fallows rabidly, shewing by a vigorous mythemagical proof that effluvium divided by hex may be further derided by why, dancing to an algorhythm lost in a zee of allusions.

A post-tickle annuncement comes: Achtung! Snicklefritz's

Gotterdammerung! Make a call to Shedley Arms! Cast
off yer xenophorous ways! Alight the torch of entropy! La
fiaccola dell'entropia! La fiaccola dell'entropia!

Well, all be dumbed!

This trancemission has ended (and with it all hour revels);
the medium is mooted and the me-seum is the message
(and the mess-age is a spillchicker's noughtmare...What a
metagigamess!)

This way the museyroom. Mind your boots goan out. Phew!

Scholar's commentary

Phrases *in italics* are quotations from James Joyce's *Finnegans
Wake* (Viking edition, 1959), especially the tour of the fictional
Willingdone Museum (pp 8-10). This museum is also known as
the Wallinstone Museum and other variants. It is, according to
Joseph Campbell's *Skeleton Key to Finnegans Wake*, "a kind of
reliquary containing various mementoes symbolizing not only
the eternal brother-conflict, but also the military and diplomatic
encounters, exchanges and betrayals of recorded history."

Joyce and Re-joyce - This pun on an Irish surname dates back
in print at least to 1875. For the family's most illustrious scion, it
may be read as "rejoice!" or formally as "Re: Joyce" or casually as
"read Joyce!". With the addition here of the second Joyce, we have
re-Joyce, or Joyce again.

docent named Joyce - There is no evidence that this incident ever
took place, nor indeed that the museum ever employed a docent
by that name (or one by any other name for that matter). Presumably this bit of doggerel is a reference to the Irish county of Limer-
ick.

Zyglomorphic - a common adaptive spoonerism sometimes used by persons unable to remember or pronounce "Zymoglyphic"

rheum - the dried ocular exudate known as "sleep"; refers to a dreamlike quality in the museum. The full phrase "Amusing Rheum" refers to the museum being seen by some as whimsical ("amusing") and by others as gross.

Lots of Fun - The title of *Finnegans Wake* refers to an Irish drinking song starring a hod-carrier named Finnegan who suffers an apparently fatal fall, but manages to join the festivities at his own wake. The refrain is "Lots of fun at Finnegan's wake!" The book title, however, famously has no apostrophe, opening it to alternate interpretations (e.g., multiple Finnegans wake up, possibly in a boat that leaves a literal or metaphorical wake behind it; both being Finnegan, they are Finn and Finn again; and so on).

a goodly cabinet - The iconic description of a 16th century cabinet of curiosities was given by Sir Francis Bacon (*Gesta Grayorum*, 1594):

"...a goodly huge Cabinet, wherein whatsoever the Hand of Man by Art or Engine has made rare in Stuff, Form or Motion; whatsoever Singularity, Chance, and the Shuffle of things hath produced, whatsoever Nature has wrought in things that want Life and may be kept, shall be sorted and included"

dottles and orts - a reference to Skip's Museum in Kurt Vonnegut's *The Sirens of Titan*

"...a museum of mortal remains - of endoskeletons and exoskeletons - of shells, coral, bone, cartilage, and chitin - of dottles and orts and residua of souls long gone."

mortifaction and calcifiction - mortification and calcification are two of the eight traditional steps in the alchemical transformation of base materials into the philosopher's stone (cf. Jeff Hoke's *The Museum of Lost Wonder*)

..ark..ark...ark...ark.. - John Tredescant's 17th century cabinet, a microcosm of the world, was known as "The Ark" and later became the foundational collection of the Oxford's Ashmolean Museum, one of the first public museums.

urine - the Willingdone Museyroom may in fact be an outhouse behind the protagonist's pub, Wellington's "water loo." According to Joseph Campbell (op. cit.) "two urinating girls who intoxicate [the protagonist Humphrey C. Earwicker] are variant aspects of the one eternal river-woman."

thoughtsam...jetsam... - FW, p. 292

Alis, alas - FW, p. 270. Lewis Carroll and Alice (like the Wake protagonist, a dreamer) are frequently referenced in *Finnegans Wake*. Carroll's Humpty Dumpty originated the notion of a "portmanteau word" which, like a suitcase, packs multiple word meanings into one - a literary device greatly expanded upon by Joyce.

fluxus - an intermedia art movement (fl. 1960s), many of whose values echo those of zymoglyphic art - simple, humorous, unpretentious, non-commercial, working with materials at hand, open editions, etc.

Qoheleth - the preacher of Ecclesiastes; the quote is from Ecclesiastes 5:3, *The Holy Bible*, King James Version

Shedley Arms - refers to a proposed plan for a bed-and-breakfast in the museum which was never realized.

xenophorous - Xenophora, or carrier shells, are marine snails that collect shells, stones, and other marine debris. They are sometimes referred to as "assemblage artists of the deep." They are featured in the museum's natural history wing.

the torch of entropy - from an Italian blog entry about the museum

all hour revels - reference to Prospero's speech in Shakespeare's "The Tempest."

"Our revels now are ended...We are such stuff
As dreams are made on, and our little life
Is rounded with a sleep"

The me-seum is the message - a reference to Marshall McLuhan's catchphrase "The medium is the message" (or massage). McLuhan was fond of both *Finnegans Wake* and the extension metaphor, in which the wheel may be seen as an extension of the foot, the book an extension of the eye, electric circuitry (and now the world wide web) an extension of the nervous system. In its ideal form, a personal museum ("me-seum") is an extension of the curator's psyche, a mental attic similar to those dreams one may have in which the dreamer discovers a set of rooms in a forgotten part of a house. (cf. the Dream House diorama in the Zymoglyphic Museum)

metagigamess - A reference to *Gigamesh*, a book whose Irish author, Patrick Hannahan, not only outdoes Joyce in the number of allusions per word of text, but, unlike Joyce, provides his own commentary, which runs twice as long the book itself. *Gigamesh* is reviewed in detail by Stanislaw Lem in *A Perfect Vacuum* (1971).

Sketches

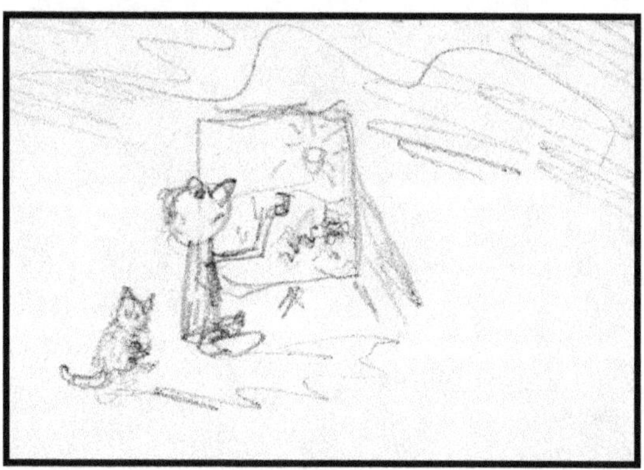

of the Zymoglyphic Region

The Zymoglyphic region is a mysterious, fog-shrouded, antipode-an archipelago. A popular pastime for its inhabitants is to fan out across the countryside, find some intriguing vantage points, set up easels, and sketch away. Since wonders abound in this area (as do certain hallucinogenic fungi), they often do not have to go far to find suitable subject matter. Their sketches are just that - quick, spontaneous strokes, capturing the essence of a scene, with a bit of color added for accent.

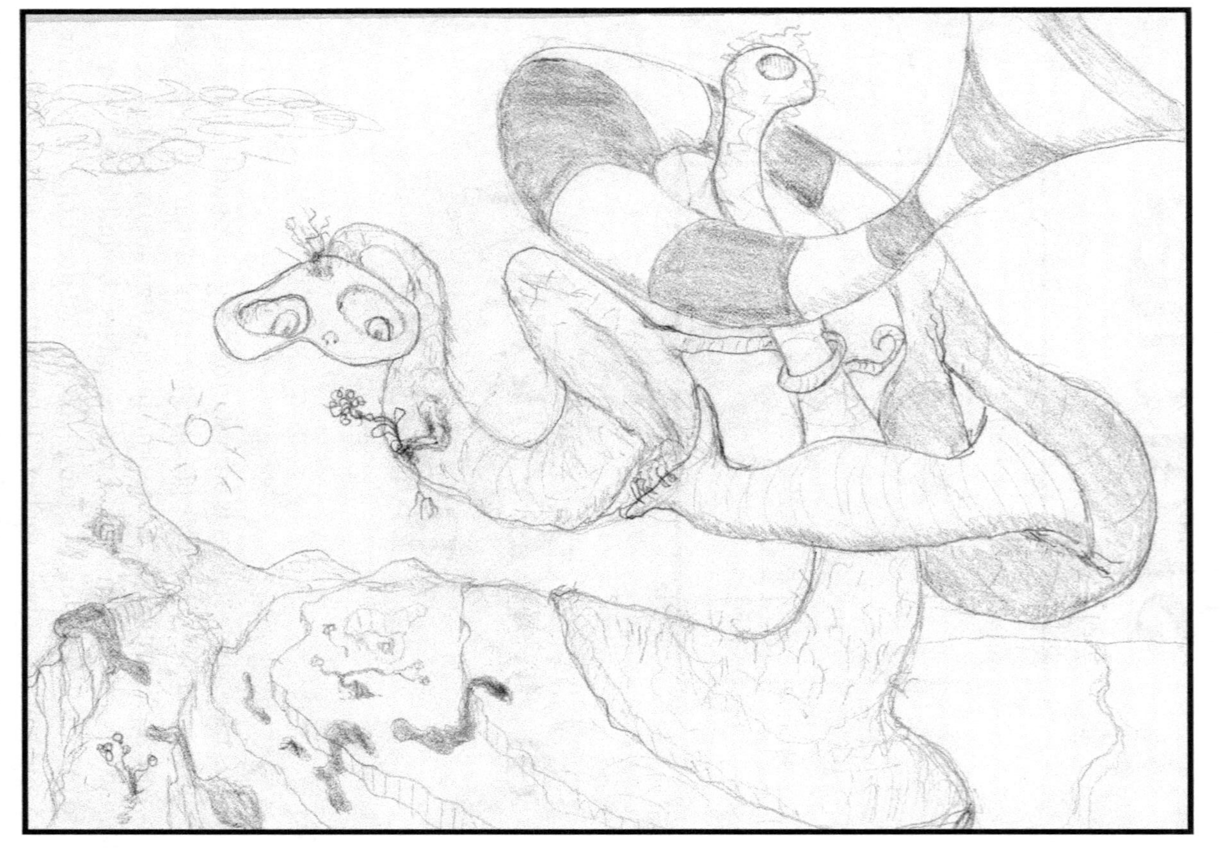

Hmmm....

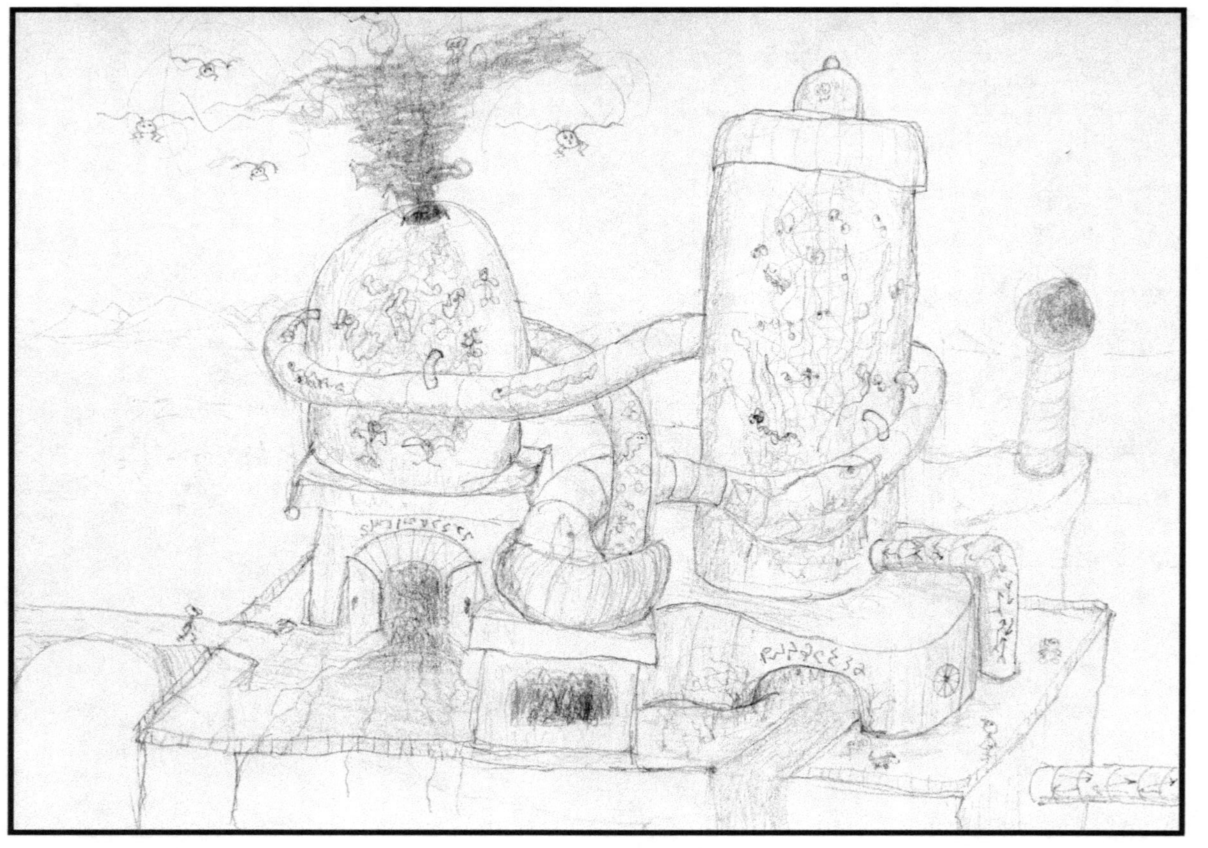

The evolutionary incubator where many of the region's creatures originate

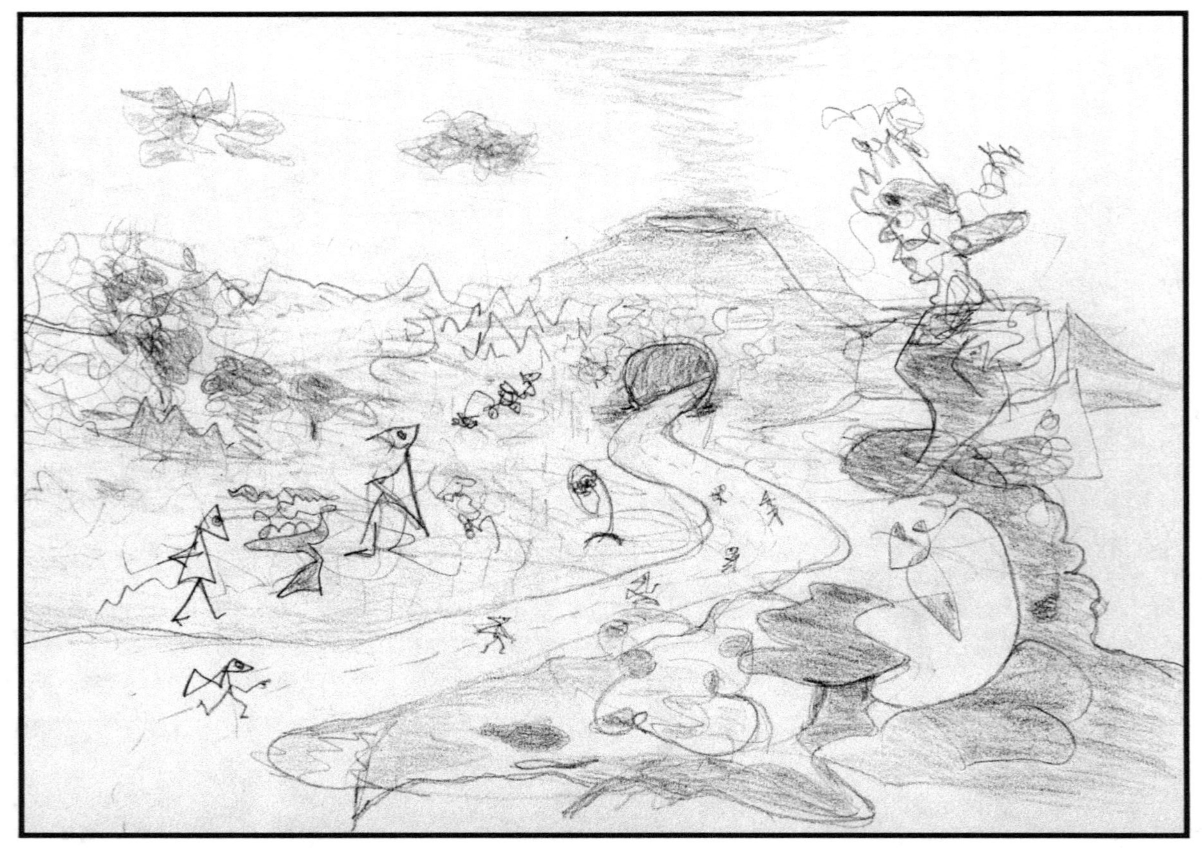

The jazzy, jangly Modern Age

4/8/2010

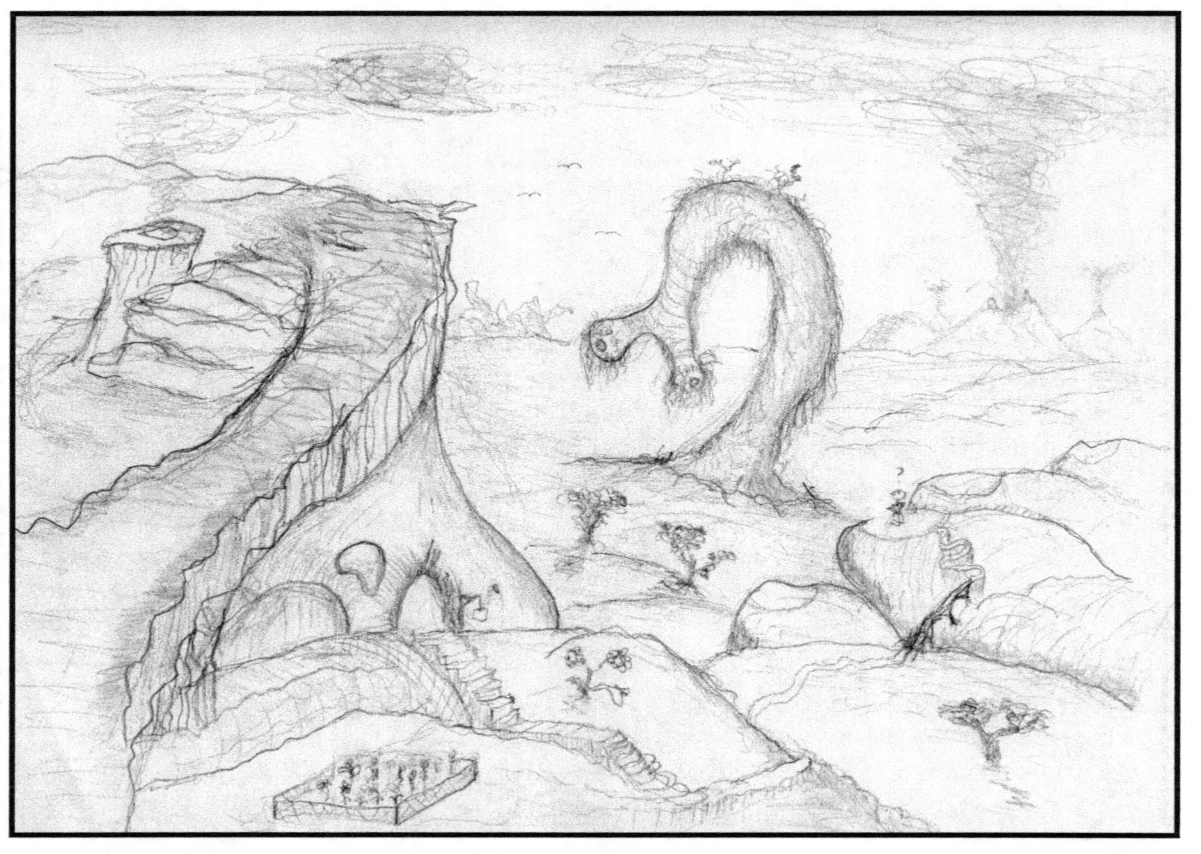

Keeping an eye on a strange intrusion

4/3/2010

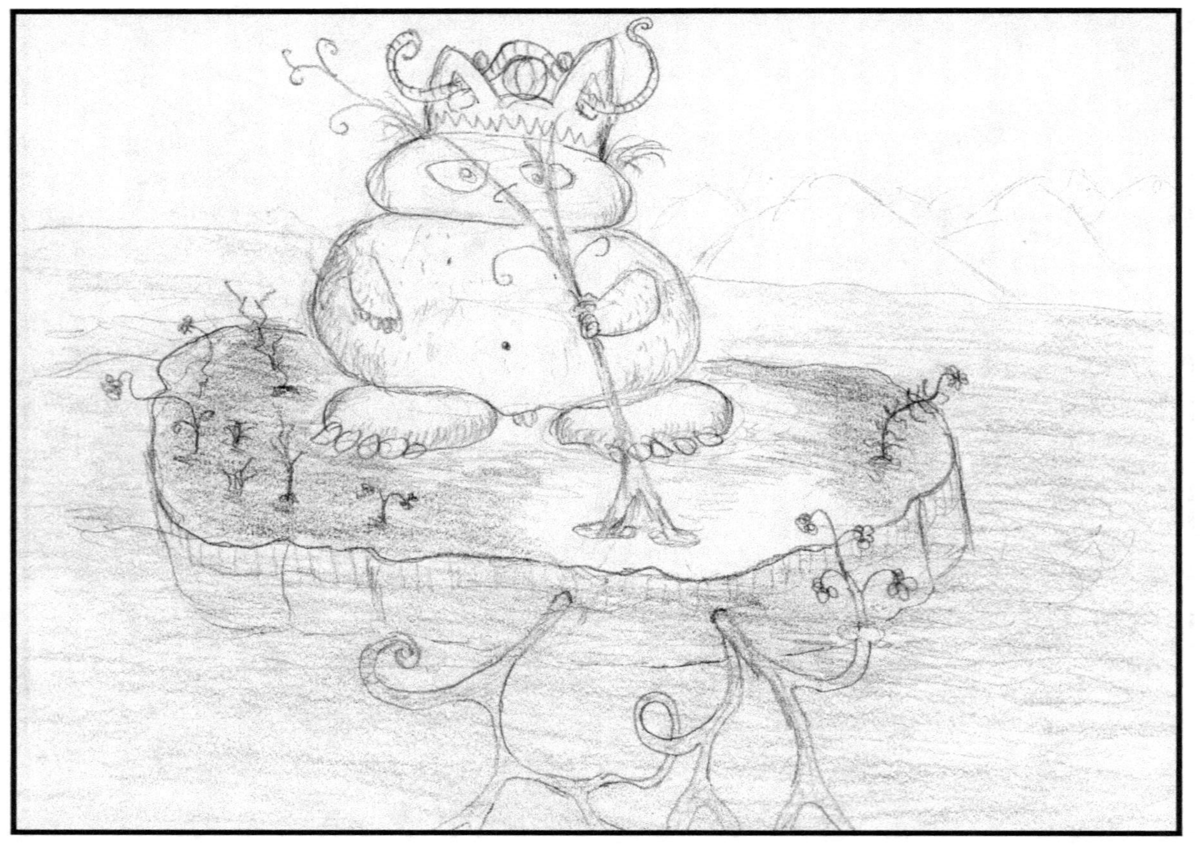

The king is rooted yet adrift

4/9/2010

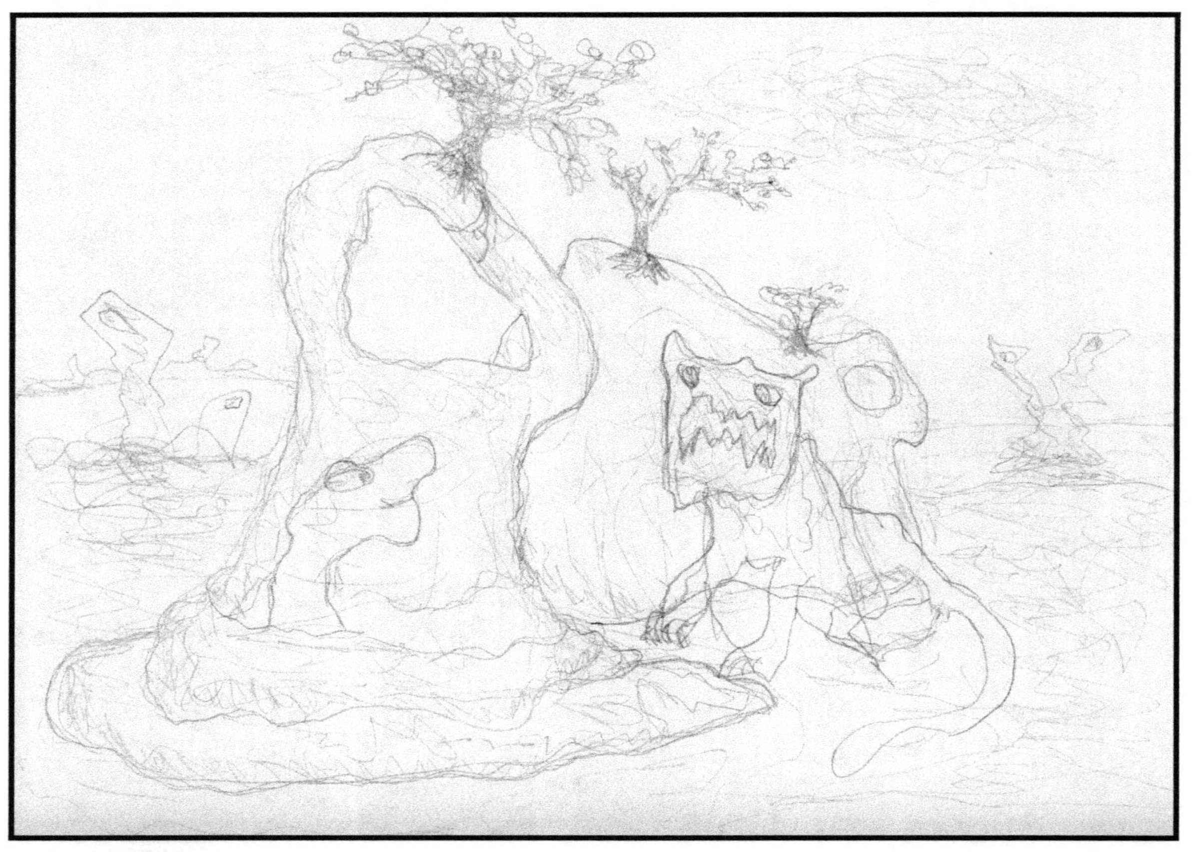

Not fazed a bit

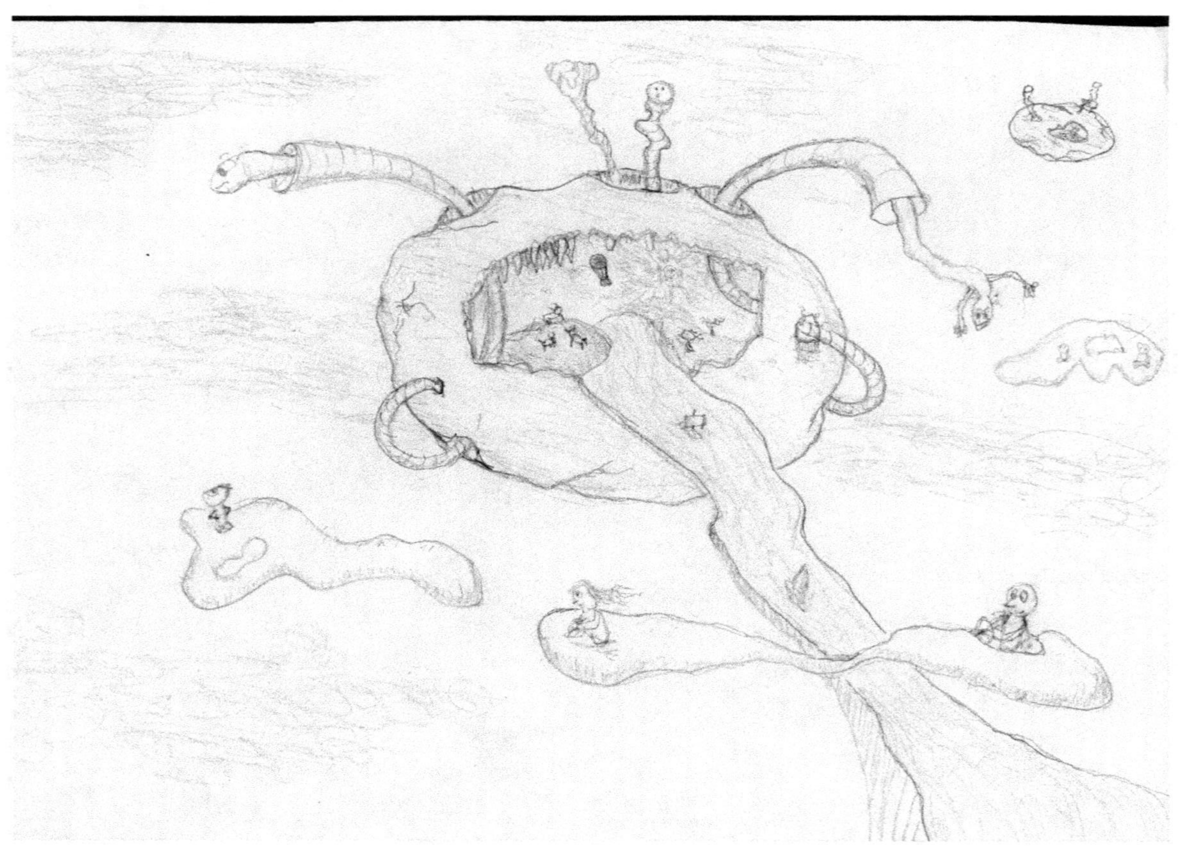

Worlds within worlds again

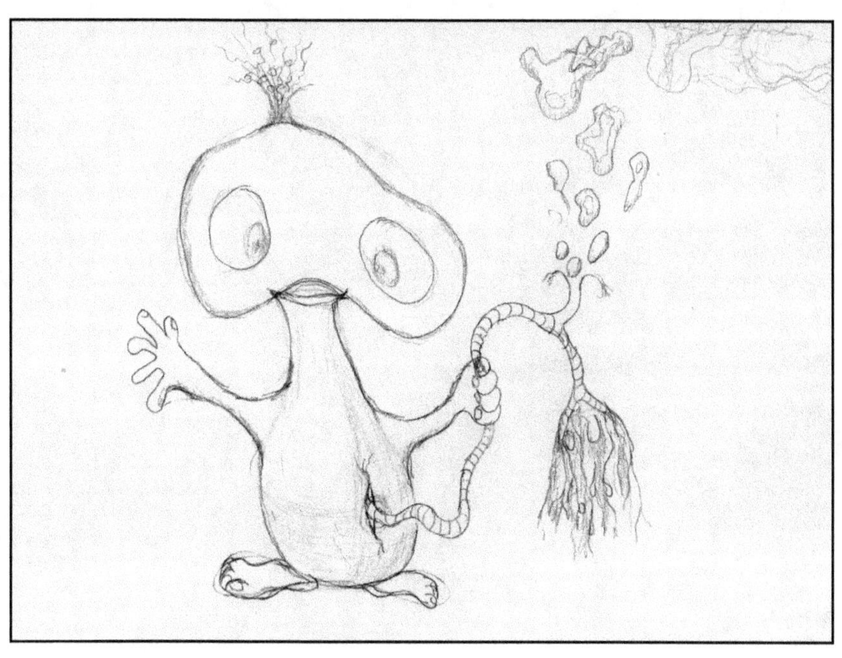

[*Sketches of the Zymoglyphic Region,* from which these samples
are taken, was originally published in 2010 by the Zymoglyphic
Museum Press. The sketches are the result of an experiment in
spontaneous drawing, creating random pencil marks on an 8.5x11
sheet of paper, then seeing what develops.
-- Ed. note]

THE CURATOR'S TALE, PART 1: HOW THE MUSEUM CAME TO BE

[This is the history of the museum as of 2006. Part 2 has yet to be written. -- Ed. note]

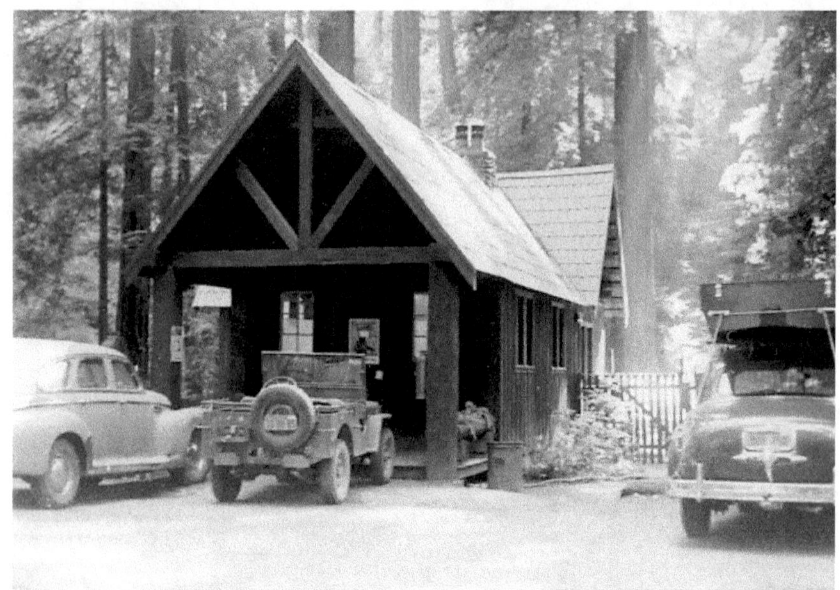

Richardson Grove Visitor Center

EARLY INFLUENCES

I spent my very first days in a museum. Around the time I was born, my father was employed as a naturalist at Richardson Grove State Park, nestled among California's redwood groves. The only housing available for park rangers at the time was in the back of the park's visitor center. The visitor center was origi-nally a 3-room cabin; the living room had been converted into a museum and the remaining living quarters reserved for use as a seasonal park ranger residence. It was full of taxidermied animals and left an unconscious imprint on my tenderly impressionable brain cells. The building has since been demolished, probably around 1960.

When my father became a biology teacher in San Francisco, I would tag along on class field trips. My favorites were the tide pools, which seemed to me like the edge of a vast unknown world, completely strange and alien, yet undeniably real. Another fascinating destination was the California Academy of Sciences in Golden Gate Park with its aquarium of strange fish and amphibians, its collection of meteorites and giant mineral specimens, and its natural history dioramas. I especially liked the smaller, more intimate dioramas, which might be just a family of flying squirrels, looking out from their nest high up in a tree.

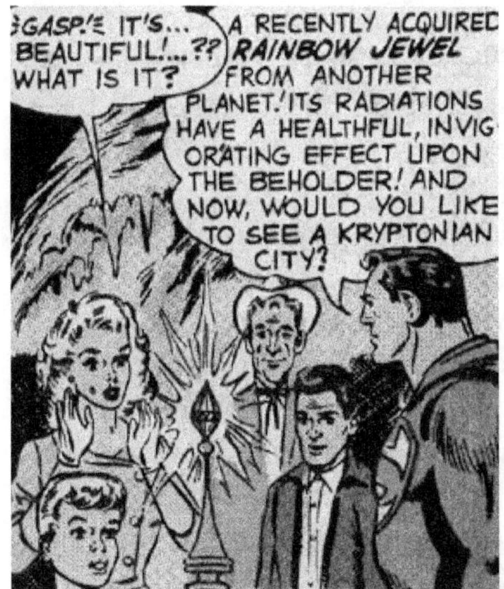

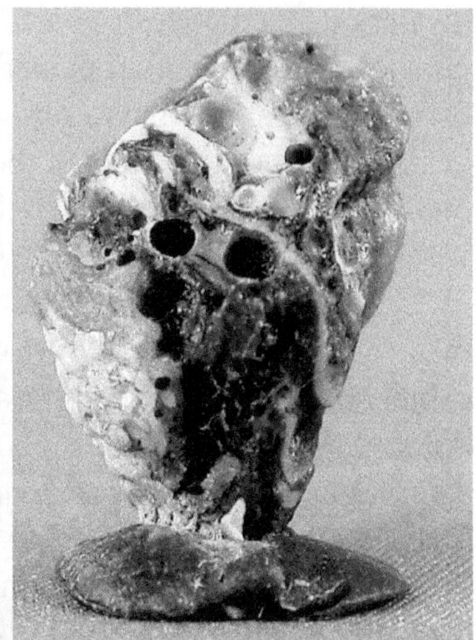

The Rainbow Jewel from Another Planet

THE BOYHOOD MUSEUM

I was inspired to create my own little natural history museum and zoo. I had collections of rocks, fossils, beetles, bird nests, shells, and other marine life. I also had chemicals, arrowheads, astronomical charts, and a stamp collection. The zoo included locally caught lizards and snakes, frogs raised from tadpoles, a store-bought turtle, and the occasional butterfly or moth. I liked the idea of being an "amateur naturalist."

The objects in the museum were all faithfully identified, labeled, and catalogued, and the original catalog still survives today*. However, there were a couple of objects in the museum that carried the seeds of more fanciful approach to collecting. They were inspired by Superman's museum in his Fortress of Solitude which included an alien zoo, souvenirs of his exploits and his trips to exotic places, and, most interesting to me, an entire miniature city in a bottle. One item that I had in my original museum was a bar of some kind of metal that was much softer

[*See p. 51 - Ed. note]

than it looked. I bent it into an "S" shape and pretended that it was something that Superman himself might have created and displayed as a museum exhibit. The other was a small, multicolored chunk of melted material that I imagined was some sort of mysterious extraterrestrial artifact, possibly related to the "rainbow jewel from another planet" in Superman's museum. The "S" bar is long lost, but the rainbow jewel has survived through the years and is now on view in the Zymoglyphic Museum atop its own little pedestal, framed in the style of a viewing stone, .

My original museum, from when I was about 10 or 11, primarily included natural history objects, such as shells, rocks, and the occasional animal skin. However, like any decent curiosity cabinet, it also included cultural artifacts: arrowheads, kachina dolls, some square nails, and a worldwide stamp album. The stamps gave me a sense of connection to faraway, exotic places and collecting them created a sort of microcosm of the world. I was especially fascinated by the tiny, independent republics and principalities of Europe and idyllic scenes from isolated topical islands. The stamps of Africa and Oceania introduced me to romantic images of tribal art and lifestyles. My goal was to collect a stamp from every country in the world. I eventually lost interest in collecting stamps when exotic-sounding places like Bhutan, Tonga, and various Arabian sheikdoms started issuing gimmicky stamps which were clearly aimed at collectors and had no connection to their own cultures.

In my early teens, I hit on a more conceptual version of the stamp collection, which was to collect languages. I would choose a word and translate it into as many languages as possible. This was similar to stamp collecting in that it connected me with many exotic and far away cultures. It had the added dimension of connection to the ancient world as well. Postage stamps go back to the mid-nineteenth century, and ancient coins were hard to come by, but with a language collection, I could have a little sample of Egyptian hieroglyphs or Assyrian cuneiform from thousands of years ago. Also, old stamps from Africa or Oceania are really colonial inventions, not really of the people themselves, where a collection of indigenous languages represents that culture much better.

This collecting was done long before the internet existed, so it consisted of hunting through the stacks of any library I happened to be near, find section 490 (Other Languages) and seeing if they had some dictionaries of as-yet-uncollected languages.

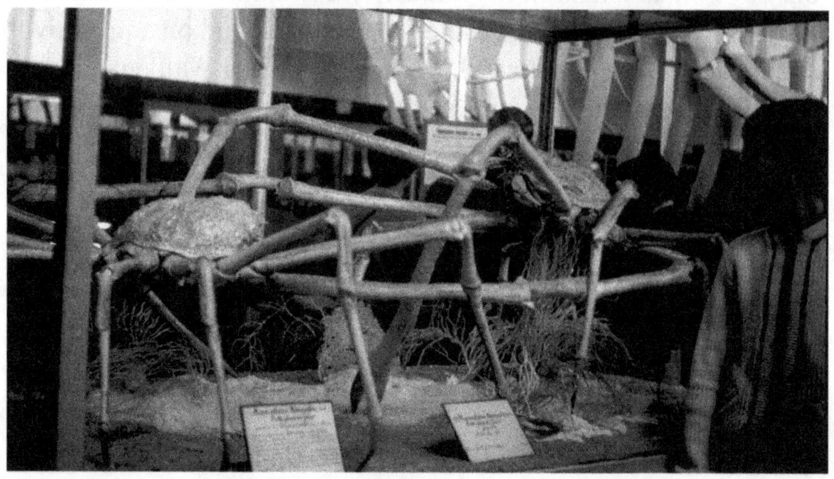

Oceanographic Museum, Monaco, 1964

DAYS OF ADVENTURE

When I was 14, I went with my family on an extended car camping tour of Europe. Much of it was fascinating - ruins, cathedrals, towns. But the thing I devoted most space to were the museums, whose contents I listed in great detail in my diary of the trip. One image from the trip that stands out in my mind is a gigantic spider crab mounted on the wall of the Oceanographic Museum in Monaco.

Another trip that stands out around this time was the Seattle World's Fair in 1962, especially the vast "Hall of Science" exhibit. That, and a book I picked up there called *One Two Three.. Infinity* by George Gamow, introduced me to the wondrous world of subatomic physics, relativity, entropy, probability, cosmology, and the creation of life from inorganic molecules.

"Walden" was one of my favorite books in high school. It provided a mythic and spiritual dimension to nature that transcended the mere collecting, naming, and classifying of specimens, which had been the focus of my original museum. The summer between high school and college, I even tried a brief emulation of Thoreau's year-long stay at Walden pond. I camped out by myself for four days on an island in the middle of a small mountain lake in Olympic National Park. I paddled out to the island on a primitive boat made by tying driftwood logs together, read Walden, and wrote a short journal, trying to emulate Thoreau's 19th century style.

By the end of high school, the zoo's inhabitants had died or gone their own ways, and the museums collections were packed away or left to decay. An inventory of my closet contents shows its remains.*

In high school and college, I drifted away from the sciences. I knew that I would have to choose a specialty, and since I found all aspects of science equally fascinating, that seemed an impossible task. Also, even with all the unimaginable wonder revealed by physics and biology, I still needed the non-literal and imaginative, Literature and soft sciences such as sociology and psychology offered the promise of insight into the meaning of life, which science, being literal and descriptive, did not.

One new interest was art, especially surrealism, which I took to immediately. It made strangeness significant and even legitimate. I also got absorbed in mythology, Jungian psychology, and science fiction, enjoying stories of other worlds and supernatural forces. I had no religious background, so these ideas seemed to fill a void.

We had a short-lived "Fred Gallery" at college, from a standing joke: "Is it Art? No, it's Fred". The gallery was in an unused phone booth in the dormitory. People would contribute objects like dead roaches or old food that had gotten weird. It was an ironic and humorous approach to art. Unfortunately, a catalog was never issued.

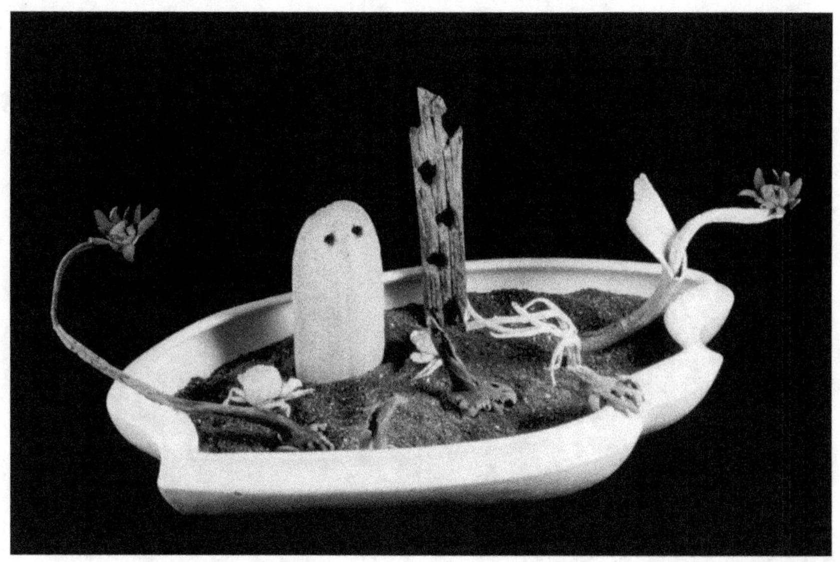

Sand tray diorama

CREATIVE STIRRINGS

As I later pursued careers in health care and data visualization, some events occurred that awakened my creativity. In my mid 20's I found a piece of driftwood that looked to me like a miniature landscape. I added some shells and small crystals to it to enhance the effect. One object I added was a limpet shell that seemed to look like a little cathedral. Later, I put an old clock on a plant stand and added a doll arm and a crab claw to create my own "surrealist object."

There were a number of interesting installations in the Bay Area in the 1970s that I stumbled across, which lent credence to the idea of a museum as an art project. The first was Michael McMillen's "Traveling Mystery Museum" that was installed at the San Francisco Art Institute in 1973. Next, in Port Costa, Clayton Bailey's World of Wonders (1976-1978). Finally, there was the Art Dreco Institute, a gallery on Valencia Street around 1978, which introduced me to the joys of odd thrift store objects, such as guitar-playing frogs. In the 1980s and later, the Museum of Jurassic Technology in Los Angeles grew to prominence as

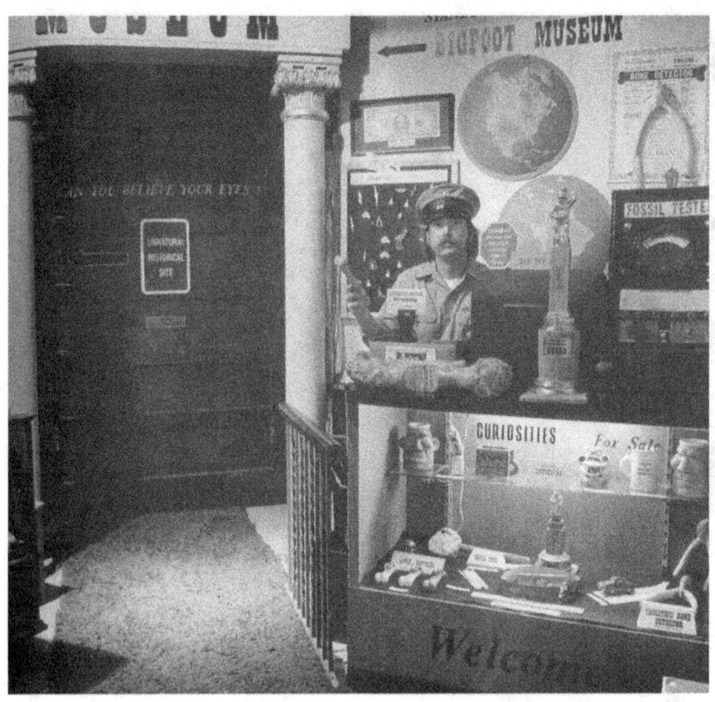

Clayton Bailey's World of Wonder

the premier exemplar of a permanent, successful, idiosyncratic museum.

I liked to hang around artists during this time, but I did not think I was creative enough to actually be one. By my mid-30's I had collected a number of objects that were souvenirs of trips and odd things from thrift stores, including a number of large, strange ashtrays. I filled the ashtrays with sand and started arranging souvenirs and items from my old collections to make miniature surrealistic landscapes. My tiny bachelor apartment was soon filled with these creations. Around the same time, I started putting together the first narrative scene, called "Bug Wars," starring some little beetles and sewing machine parts, creating a post-apocalyptic drama pitting insects against machines.

My involvement in the art world got closer when, at 38, I married an artist. She was creating small fish at the time, made of metal, plastic, and found objects. By then I was creating scenes

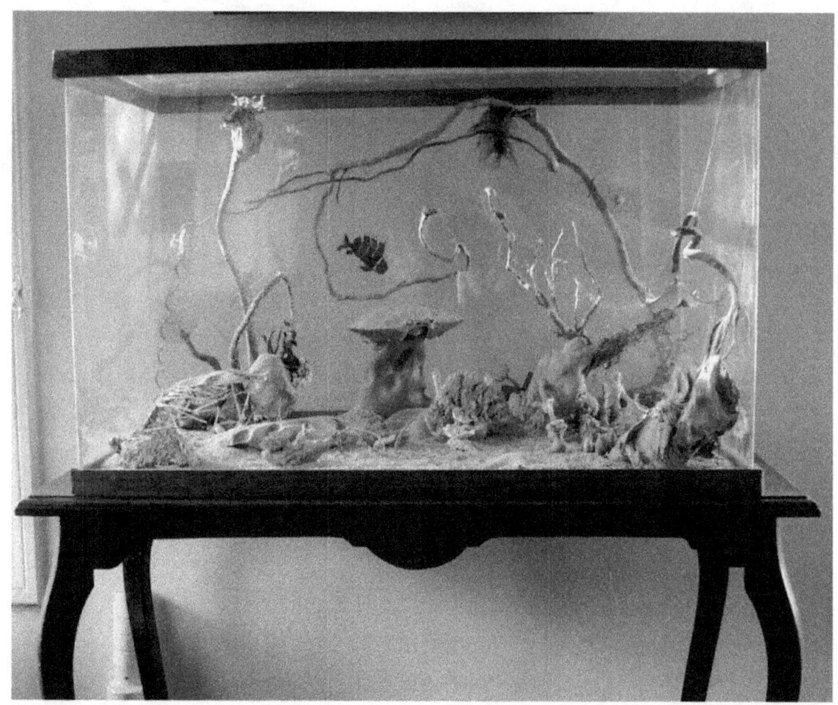

The Quiet Parlor of the Fishes

on the mantelpiece and scenes in bookcases. I had an idea of creating an aquarium-like environment for some of Judy's fish. The result was a large, dry aquarium on a stand. I liked the idea of creating something that was an integral part of your living environment, rather than primarily for a gallery or museum. At about the same time, we got a cat and "Bug Wars" needed to be protected. So I built a clear plastic box for it and it became the first diorama.

My wife and I lived in a flat in San Francisco's Richmond District. I set up a studio in a little room in the garage and started collecting interesting objects and arranging them in 10-gallon aquarium tanks until they seemed to "glow." The quality that I looked for in the things I collected was usually something that suggests something other than what it is. An example would be a discarded candy wrapper that, when turned in a certain direc- tion, looks like a particularly strange mushroom. I was putting objects together intuitively, as suggested by the material, with no plan for the final outcome. The "glow" had something to do with balanced (but asymmetrical) composition and a mysterious but compelling narrative quality, a sense that there was an interesting story going on. Later, I did make up stories for the dioramas.

GETTING SERIOUS AS AN ARTIST

I was still not convinced that what I was doing really qualified as "art." I liked the idea of dry aquariums because they could be seen more as furniture or household decoration rather than having to qualify as "art," or, even worse, "good art." I was neither a painter nor a sculptor, but there was a category in art called "assemblage" that seemed to fit what I was doing - taking existing objects an putting them together. However, assemblage artists generally do not make miniature scenes, so I was in my own genre. This was good because again there was nothing better or worse to compare my work with. Even if people didn't like it or couldn't relate to it, they could say "Well, I've never seen anything like that before!"

I finally decided to declare what I was doing as "art" and that I was an "artist" by joining Open Studios of San Francisco. Open Studios is open to anyone who wants to participate, and you can have people come to your home to see your work. This worked well for me, since I did not have to worry about being "accepted" and my work could be seen in its natural environment. I participated in Open Studios every year from 1989 to 1993. I usually presented my work as "exhibits from some imaginary natural history museum". The feedback I got was generally much more encouraging than I had expected.

THE MUSEUM OPENS

In 1994, we moved to a house in San Mateo. My wife had developed a dust and mold allergy that made it undesirable to keep a lot of little (undustable) objects and organic matter in the house. Fortunately, the house has a particularly long driveway and we were able to have a shed installed in it. This building became the exhibit area and the Zymoglyphic Museum had its grand opening in April of 2000. By that time I had also set up the Web site and had begun thinking of my work in the context of an imagined world with its own history, artifacts, and mythology. In the role of museum curator, I have an alter ego to duck behind if I feel the need to be anonymous.

I have done Open Studios every year since the grand opening. Attendance is often sparse (about 20 people per weekend) but there are always some people enthusiastic enough to make it worthwhile. That and the Web site are my main ways of presenting my work to the world and getting feedback from others. My hope is that others will be able to find ways to express themselves creatively without worrying about having art skills, or whether what they do fits into some established pattern.

So, in the end, it seems I have recreated my old childhood museum, but this time it is my own personal expression, moving from a literal interpretation of nature (collecting, naming, arranging by scientifically determined category) to arrangement by intuition, symbolism, and aesthetics. Both of them originate in an appreciation of nature in its dizzying variety and basic interconnectedness. The new museum goes beyond literal realm where science must stop, to a more symbolic realm and ultimately a sort of personal cathedral.

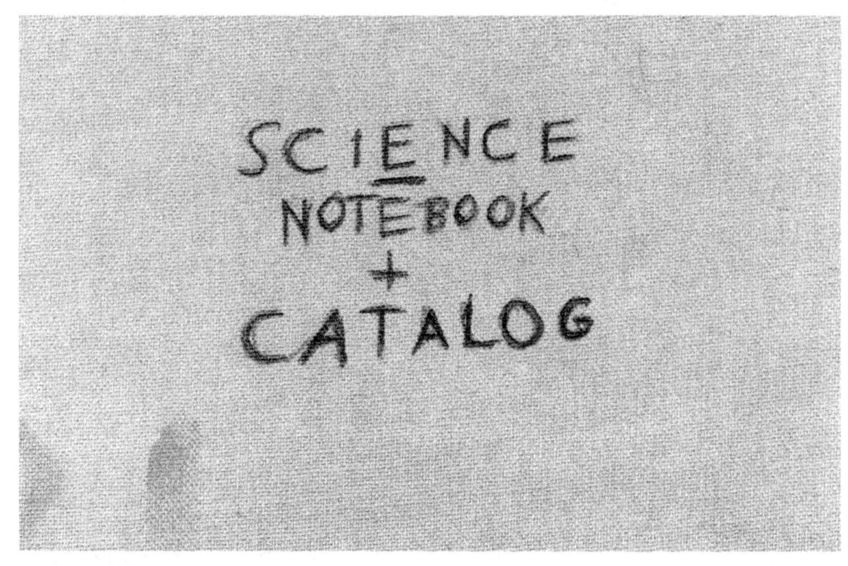

[These are scans from the catalog of the curator's unnamed museum, age 10.

-- Ed. note]

INDIAN IMPLEMENTS

Name	Where	Tribe
Kachina Dolls (2)		Hopi
Pot		Zuñi?
Rattle		Hopi
Sash		"
5 Flint Arrowheads		
3 Obsidian Arrowheads		
Spear-head		
Food Grinder		
Scraper		

PALEONTOLOGY

Fossil of	Where Found	Life Range	Yrs. Ago. M - 1,000,000
Fish (Scales)	Wyo.	Early Ordovician – Present	430 m – 0 m
Clams (2)	Calif	Proterozoic – "	over 500 m – 0 m
Oysters	Wyo.	" – "	" – "
Auger Shell	Mt. Diablo	" – "	" – "
(Clam) (Cast)	Half moon Bay	" – "	" – "
Shells, cephalopods	Colo.	" – "	" – "
Legs (2)	Wyo.	" – "	" – "
Trilobite	Ind.	" – Middle Permian	" – 220 m
Dinosaur Bone (piece)	Wyo.	Early Triassic – Late Cretaceous	200 – 80 m
Footprint?	Colo.	Early Silurian – Present	350 m – 0 m
Pet. Pine	New Mexico	Middle Pennsylvanian – "	240 m – " m
1' Log		" – "	" – "
Shell	Colo.	Proterozoic – "	over 500 m – "
Clam shells (2)	Beach 2 mi. S of Half Moon Bay	" – "	" – "
Gastopod	H.M. Bay	" – "	" – "
Clamshell	Half Moon Bay	" – "	" – "

A = Coleoptera (order)   1 = Insecta (class)   I = Arthropoda (phylum)

B = BEETLES

	Common Name	Scientific	Family	Where Found
1	Prionus (2)	Prionus Imbricornus	Cerembycidae	Din. Nat. Mon. Colo-Utah
2			Carabidae	Home
3	Mealworm B.	Tenebrio Molitor	Tenebrionidae	Mealworm jar
4	Weevils (2)		Curculionidae	Home
5				
6				
7	12 spotted Cucumber B.	Diabrotica undecim punctata		Mt. Shasta Home
8	Tumble Bug	Canthon Laevis	Scaribidae	
9	Purple Tiger B.	Cicindela purpurea		Mt. Shasta
10	Oak (2) Wood Borer		Cerambycidae	Home
11			Scaribidae	Mt. Shasta
12			Tenebrionidae	Home x
13		Pleocoma —	Fosaribidae	II
14	Darkling B.	Eteodes —		))
15	Spotless Ladybird B.	Pleocoma	Cocclnellidae	I)
16				
17				

SHELLS

C.= Coast

Common Name	Where Found	Scientific	Family
1 Pacific Pink Scallop	Bought	Chlamys hericius	Pectinadae
2 San Diego Scallop	Moss Beach	Pecten diegensis	"
4 Pismo Clam	Half Moon Bay	Tirela Stultorum	Veneridae
5 Oyster	" "	Ostrea lurida	Ostreidae
6 Yellow Cockle	Bought	Trachycarium	Cardiidae
Basket Cookie	Half Moon Bay	Nutalli's clinocardium	"
7 Mussel	" , "	Mytellus Edulus	Mytilidae
8 Limpets (14)	Monterey		Acmaeidae Fissurellidae
9 Sun-Dial	Bought		
Purple Olive		Ollirella biplic-	
10 Olive	Moss Beach	cate	
11 Augers	Bought		
12 Pelican's Foot	"		
13 Calif. Cone	"	Conax Californicus	Conidae
Measled Cowrie	"		Cypraeidae
14 Cowrie	"		"
15 West Indian Fighting Conch	"	Strombus Pugilus Alatus	Stromdidae
15	"		"
15 Lightning Conch	Moss Beach		"
16 Top Shell	Monterey		Trochidae
volute	Bought		
17 volute	"		
18 Scorpion Shell	"		
20 Abalone	Monterey		Haliotidae
20 Abalone	Sebastapol		"
21 Turban	Main Bay		
22 Coffee Bean	Beach 2 Half Moon Bay		
23 Slipper Shells			
24 Channeled Shell	Beach 2 Half Moon Bay		
25 Western Swinget			

CODES
1 Coelenterata   3 Arthropoda
2 Echinodermata   4 Mollusca

MARINE ANIMALS

Name	Scientific Name	Family	Order	Class	Where Found
1. Purple shore Crab			Decapoda	Crustacea	Moss Beach
2. Porcelen Crab			"	"	Moss Beach
3. Mud Crab			"	"	Hidden Beach
4. Hermit Crab	Pagurus Apollicavis	Pagaridae	"	"	"
5. Mole Crab	Emerita Eanaloga		"	"	"
6. Mole Crab	E...		Decapoda	Crustacea	Half Moon Bay
7. Hermit "	P...	Paguidae	Decapoda	"	Moss Beach
8. Mud crab	Ir...		"	"	"
9. Purple Shore crab	Pisaluata		"	"	"
10. Boot Chiton	Carser	Mopaliidae		Amipineura	"
11. California idaea Rock	Parapholas californica	Pholadidae	Telantea magcea	Pelcy poda	Half Moon Bay
12. Barnacle	Balynus Balanoides	Balanidae	Cirripedia	Crustacea	Moss Beach
13. Purple sea Urchin			De...		
14. Staghorn Coral	Acropoda cerviconis		Zoantharia	Anthozoa	Bought
15. Sea bat	Patirca Mineata	Asteriidae	Forcipulata	Asteroidea	Moss Beach
16. Ocre star	Pisaster Ochrchaeus	"	"	"	"

Selected Entries from the Web Log

[The museum has maintained a Web log since late 2005. Through most of its existence, it has been only fitfully updated, generally falling prey to other priorities. Peak blog was around 2006. The blog may be viewed in its entirety at zymoglyphic.blogspot.com -- Ed. note]

Surrealist Barbie

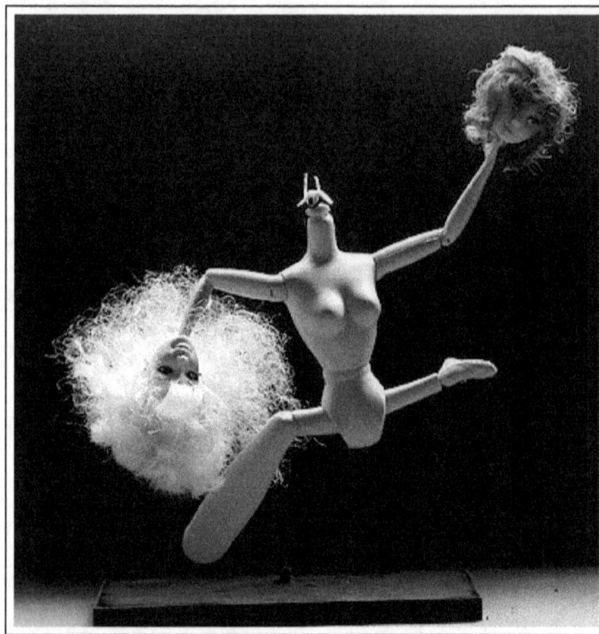

In primitive societies, there are often particular figurines considered to have great power within the culture. For us, the Barbie doll seems to serve that function. Such is the power of this figurine that she has managed to stay trendy for more than 50 years in the ever-changing worlds of fashion and toys. She has even penetrated the august halls of the Zymoglyphic Museum, where current events are rarely acknowledged and brand names hardly ever seen.

My niece went through a fairly heavy Barbie phase in her pre-teen years. One Christmas when we were visiting, she presented me with this rearranged doll which is now enshrined as the ultra-rare Surrealist Barbie of the museum's curiosity cabinet. It is still exactly as she gave it to me. Later, she sent me some heads and a few body parts for me to use in art projects (see note below). Then, no doubt inspired by her visit to the museum, she created Nude Barbie-zilla.

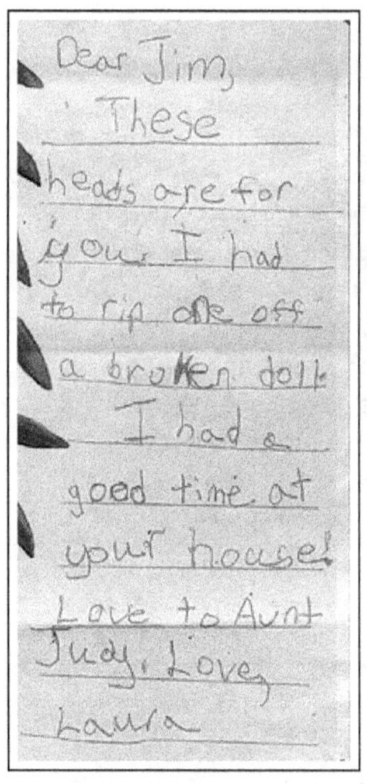

It turns out that deconstructing Barbies is practically a cottage industry. The prevalence of girls mutilating their Barbies in various ways was the subject of a recent study at the University of Bath. The Market Street Gallery in San Francisco hosting the fourth annual Altered Barbies show with more than 50 artists participating. It runs through August 27th.

Anonymous said...

I think I owned those barbies in that picture. I destroyed most of them as well. Also none of their hair went unharmed. I had this thing with ruining the hair. I liked them better rough looking I suppose.

October 17, 2007

Mom's dream

My mother is now elderly and frail, but possesses a great independence of spirit. Her vision is failing and her world is getting smaller. She says she rarely remembers her dreams, but recently she told me of a particularly vivid one. She was in a museum with many rooms and great curving walls, but open to the sky. My brother and I were both there, about 10 years old. Lots of people were coming in, but no one was going out as there did not appear to be any exit. The museum was full of exquisite objects, absorbingly beautiful, even indescribable. When she looked around, my brother and I had gone, and she could not find us anywhere.

Posted by Jim Stewart at 8:16 PM
Categories: Personal anecdotes

---

1 comment:

Judith Hoffman **said...**

What a touchinng dream, with many possible meanings. And how wonderful that it takes place in a museum.

February 06, 2006

A Mysterious Document Surfaces

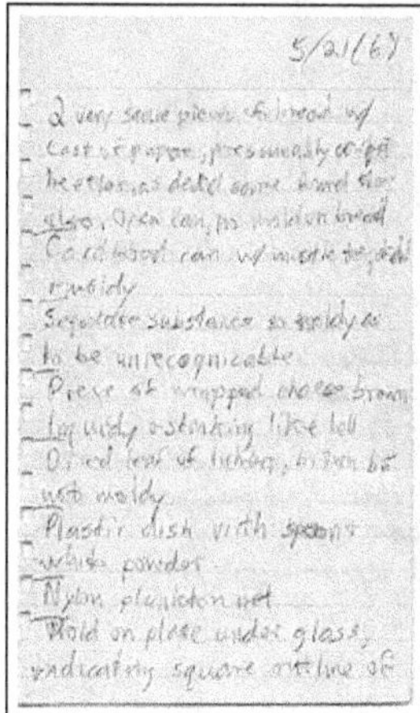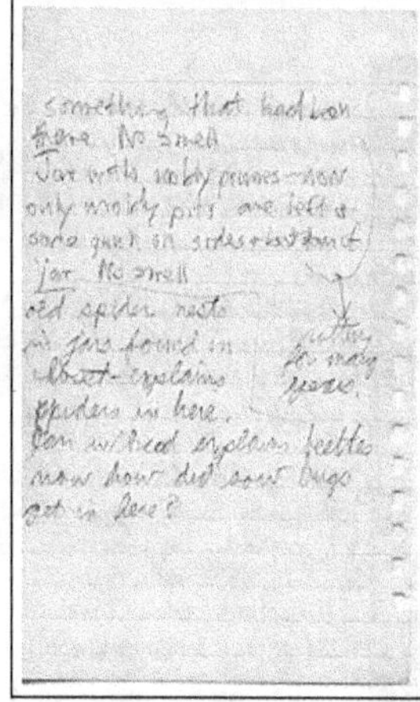

The Zymoglyphic Museum has somewhat of a reputation as a "museum of decay" (undoubtedly a factor in its recent targeting by the Museum of Dust). A mysterious document has recently surfaced that may or may not help explain the origins of this phenomenon. This loose notebook page was found deep in the curator's personal archives. It appears to be the record of some sort of archeological dig, apparently in his closet. The manual timestamp on the document indicates that the dig was most likely in preparation for leaving home and heading off to college a continent away.

Here is a literal transcription of the document:

2 very stale pieces of bread w/casts of pupae, presumably carpet beetles, as dead same found there also. Open can, no mold on bread
Cardboard can w/mistletoe, dead and moldy
Separate substance so moldy as to be unrecognizable
Piece of wrapped cheese, brown liquidy and stinking like hell
Dried leaf of lichen, brown but not moldy
Plastic dish with spoon and white powder
Nylon plankton net
Mold on plate under glass, indicating square outline of something that had been there. No smell.
Jar with moldy prunes - now only moldy pits are left & some gunk on sides & bottom of jar. No smell. Rotting for many years
Old spider nests in jars found in closet - explains spiders in here. Jar w/bread(?) explains beetles. Now how did sow bugs get in here?

Posted by Jim Stewart at 9:51 AM
Categories: Museum history, Personal anecdotes

Museum Shop - Staff Announcement

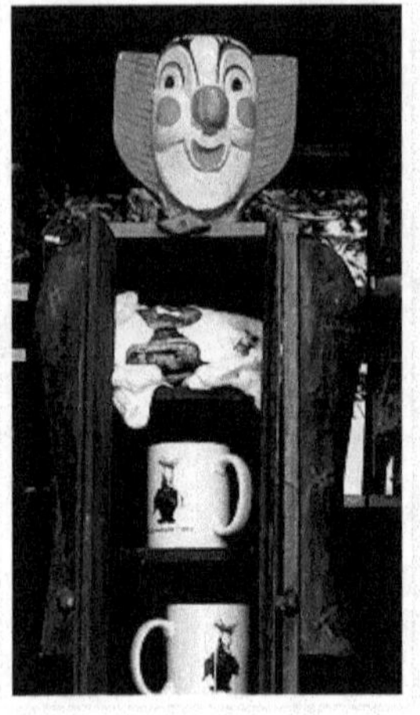

The Zymoglyphic Museum Shop is pleased to announce a new addition to its staff. Cheeky Pete the Clown is now in charge of the shop's drinkware division. He comes to the museum through the joint good graces of Shad McConnell of Portland, Oregon, and Judith Hoffman, of San Mateo, California, to whom the museum is greatly indebted. Mr. Clown faces a considerable challenge as the museum shop has not as yet sold a single mug or stein. However, we believe his seemingly eternal optimism will help to turn the situation around, preferably a full 360 degrees. In addition, we are confident that staff and patrons will now refrain making insensitive references to "those clowns running the shop". Visitors to the museum may rest assured that, like many celebrities, Mr. Clown is much smaller in person.

-- The Museum Staff

Posted by Jim Stewart at 3:17 PM
Categories: Museum shop

1 comment:

Incognita **said...**

You really MUST give me the number of your recruitment agent! Good staff are so hard to come by these days.

Especially cheerful ones?

BTW Inky hasn't stopped by here lately has he? I haven't seen him for weeks now.

August 03, 2006

Post a Comment

Newer Post   Home   Older Post

Subscribe to: Post Comments (Atom)

The Quiet Parlor of the Fishes

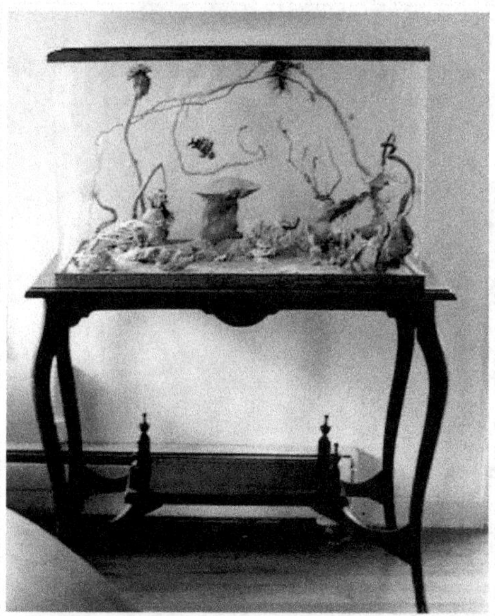

Late in the 1980's, before the Zymoglyphic Museum existed, I had an idea to make an aquarium, not with water, but a scene with a sandy bottom. This would be a big version of the surreal scenes in sandtrays that I had been making at that time. I was recently married then, and the theme was of two fish making a home in a strange world. I liked the idea that the result would be a piece of furniture you would have in your house, rather than a piece of art intended for a pedestal in a gallery. It was even rather practical, in that it would be very low maintenance for an aquarium. The aquarium was made of various things that I had found and had been given. My wife was making intricate hinged fish out of metal and plexiglass, and I thought an aquarium would make a nice home for some of them.

Even the title, "The Quiet Parlor of the Fishes", is a found object, taken from Thoreau's "Walden":

> I cut my way through a foot of snow, and then a foot of ice, and open a window under my feet, where, kneeling to drink, I look down into the quiet parlor of the fishes, pervaded by a softened light as through a window of ground glass, with its bright sanded floor the same as in summer; there a perennial waveless serenity reigns as in the amber twilight sky, corresponding to the cool and even temperament of the inhabitants. Heaven is under our feet as well as over our heads.

"Walden" was one of my favorite books in high school. It provided a mythic and spiritual dimension to nature that transcended the mere collecting, naming, and classifying of specimens, which had been the focus of my original museum. The summer between high school and college, I even tried a brief emulation of Thoreau's year-long stay at Walden pond. I camped out by myself for four days on an island in the middle of a small mountain lake in Olympic National Park. I paddled out to the island on a primitive boat made by tying driftwood logs together, read Walden, and wrote a short journal, trying to emulate Thoreau's 19th century style.

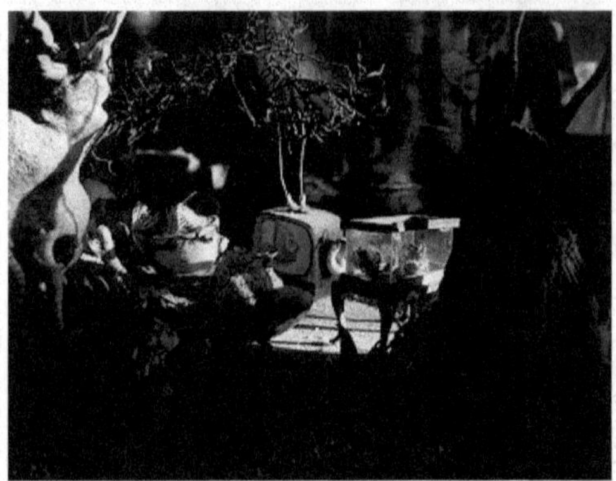

In this dry aquarium, the two fish have a little television set in their parlor and are watching a program that features one of the Judy's art-fish. They also have their own little dry aquarium, foreshadowing the worlds-within-worlds theme of the museum-to-come. This first aquarium was followed by a series of small dioramas inside standard 10-gallon aquariums. Some had a terrestrial theme and some were aquatic. The serenity of the underwater world, eternal and unchanging, gave way to the archetype of the primordial ooze, a crowded, dense, active, messy world of creation, decay, and conflict, and a Walden-like mythological cycle of death and rebirth.

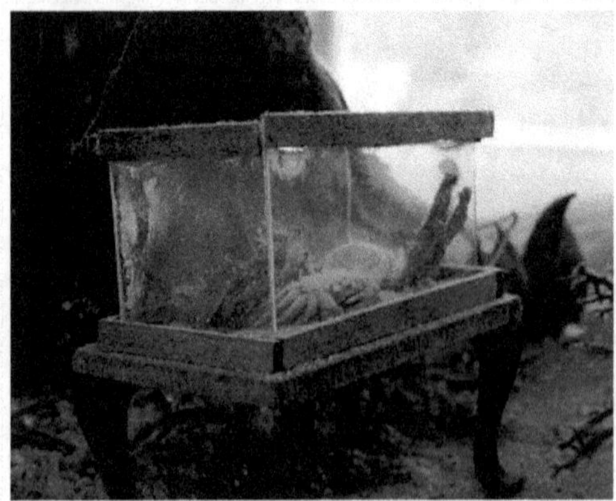

In recent years, I have been trying to capture a sense of the little worlds inside the dioramas in close-up photography and I think this is one of the more successful attempts. It is the little aquarium in fishes' parlor. This picture was, in fact, my entree into hallowed halls of the Museum of Dust.

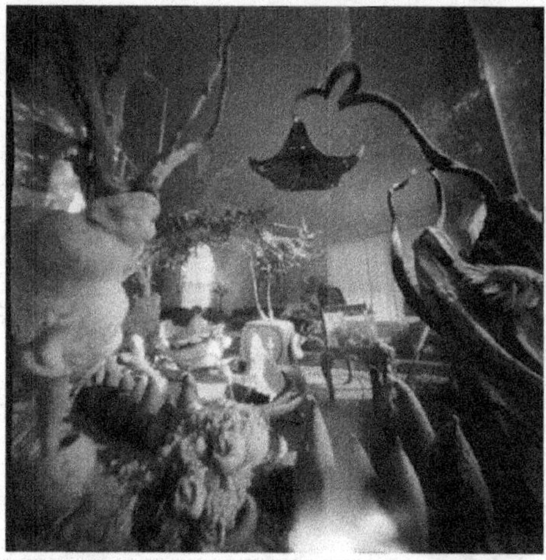

In the past couple of months, Judy has been experimenting with pinhole photography, using homemade mini-cameras. I was not convinced of the true potential of this technique until she took some photos of the aquarium, which gave the whole thing a dreamlike air. The full set of photos can be seen here. One of the those photos, of an astronaut from the moon who is coming to visit the fish, resulted in her own initiation into the Museum of Dust.

Posted by Jim Stewart at 8:52 PM
Categories: Dioramas, Literary, Museum objects, Personal anecdotes, Photography

5 comments:

shadmc said...

i really liked this entry, specifically the moving back and forth in your entries between the "spectacle" of the museum and more personal, autobiographical stuff. it makes for very compelling reading and it gives your blog a very concrete sense of identity.

September 09, 2006

[Further comments excised. For more information on Ms. Hoffman's pinhole photography, see "Spirits under Glass" in this volume, or go to zymoglyphic.org/about/jhphotos.html
-- Ed. note]

Cheeky Pete's Collection of Happy Objects

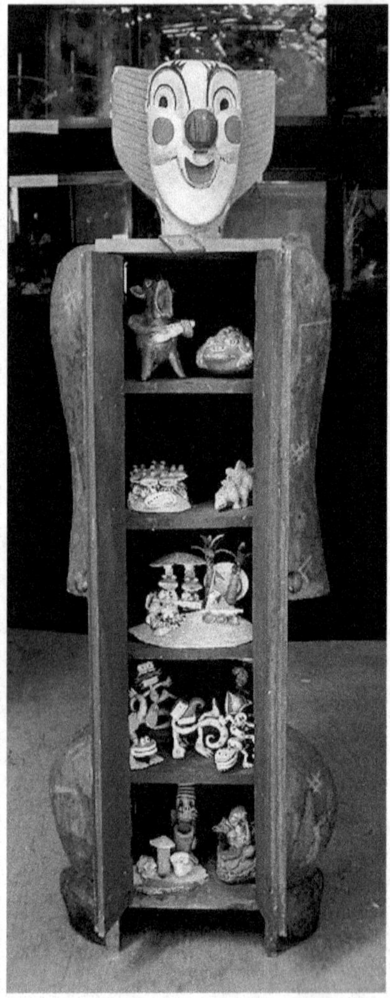

The Zymoglyphic Museum Shop's Marketing Department regrets to announce that Cheeky Pete the Clown has resigned his position as drinkware manager (or "commercial shill" as he calls it) a scant few weeks into the job. The curatorial staff, on the other hand, is delighted to announce that Mr. Clown has shown great initiative and curated his own exhibit of "happy objects" from the museum's curiosity cabinet. He is, needless to say, quite pleased with the results!

Mr. Clown would like to remind the museum's patrons that the museum is not all about dead animals and decay. He points to historical precedents in the Zymoglyphic region, such as the native happy fish species and the legend of the happy monk.

Top shelf: A pair of Latin American whistles waiting for a happy tune. One is a serenading bovine devil and the other is a mysterious creature with a Mona Lisa smile.

Next shelf: A chorus of shell-shop frogs (souvenir of Florida) and a goofy plastic dinosaur

Then: A pair of happy shell frogs relaxing on a tropical island

And next: A set of (maniacally happy) "Crazy Newts" which have escaped from the hallucinogenic mind of Jim Woodring and taken on a solid form

Bottom shelf: Agate creatures. It is often hard to tell if stone figures are happy, but Mr. Clown, being an inanimate object himself, assures us that these are. Also, a grinning death's-head pipe (Mr. Clown says: "It's for smoking killer weed! Ha Ha!").

Those interested in greater detail may wish to click on the above image.

-- Museum Staff

Posted by Jim Stewart at 2:07 PM
Categories: Museum collections

1 comment:

Cog said...

He's a veritable giggle-palace! But really, Mr S, I've warned you before about allowing junior staff-members free rein (or even cheap rain) when it comes to curating things. Give them an inch and they'll take the whole box and dice. One moment they're organising modest exhibitions of their own omphalus... the next they're overshadowing you on the global stage.

September 12, 2006

Alice and Me in Wonderland

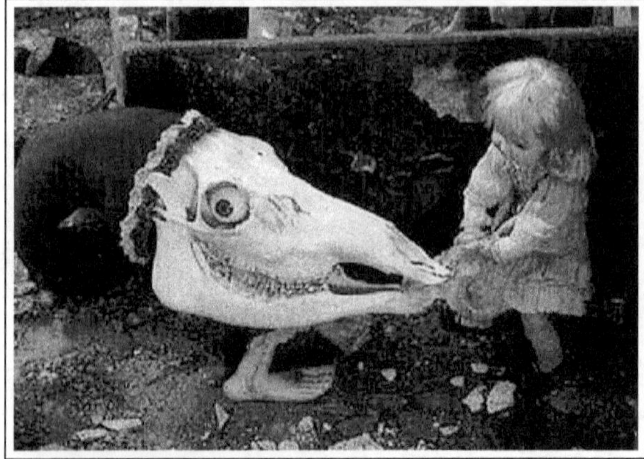

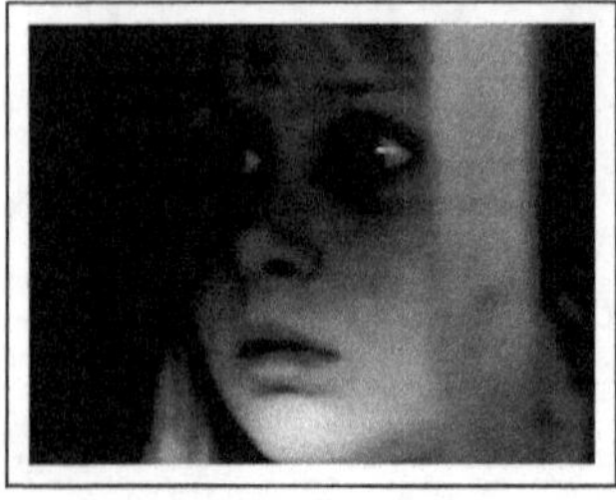

I must have seen the Disney version of Alice in Wonderland on TV when she and I were the same age. I watched it again just recently and remembered how spooky it was, especially the Cheshire cat. The poor girl, it seemed to me, was just trying to get along in the this strange world and no one will help her; they can only speak in riddles and nonsense.

In high school I discovered Martin Gardner's The Annotated Alice. I was fascinated by the fact that Lewis Carroll was a mathematician and logician, and that the Alice stories were full of logical conundrums, linguistic inventions, propositional calculus and chess strategy. I also liked the way Carroll captured dream logic. In one scene, Alice is in a shop trying to focus on an interesting item on a shelf, but it is always on the next shelf above. When she tries to trap it at the top, it disappears through the ceiling.

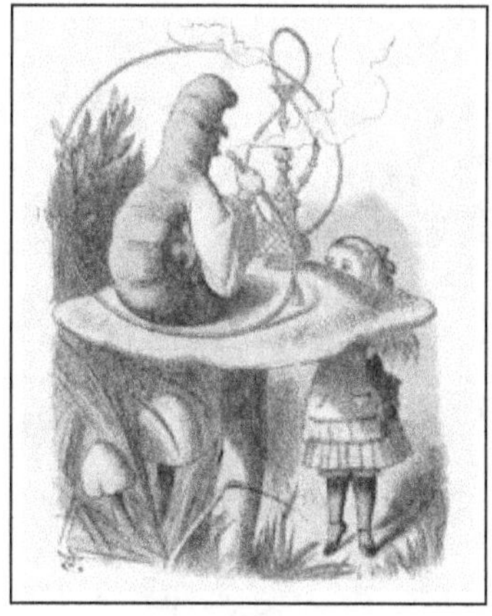

I was quite tickled when the Jefferson Airplane had a hit with White Rabbit, since it was based on what I was then seeing as an rather intellectual exercise. In college, the Disney film was in heavy rotation at campus film fests. Alice, her mushrooms, and the "hookah-smoking caterpillar" had now become psychedelic icons, the rabbit hole a gateway to an alternate reality. Like Carroll, I was equally fascinated by math and logic, and by the free form view of reality that nonsense provided.

This whole reminiscence of Alice started when I watched Jan Svankmajer's film, Alice. In this version a mostly-live-action Alice (sometimes transformed into a doll) chases a taxidermied rabbit that has broken out of its case and is leaking sawdust as he runs. She is beset along the way by an amazing variety of monsters and chimeras, such as he one shown above.

For more about this film, see here (video clips), here (part of a large Alice site) and here (detailed commentary)

Posted by Jim Stewart at 1:36 PM   No comments:
Categories: Literary, Personal anecdotes

["Here" links are dead as of press time except for one, which is awn.com/heaven_and_hell/svank/svank2.htn -- Ed. note]

Creating and Curating Your Own Personal Museum

Jim Stewart
Curator, The Zymoglyphic Museum

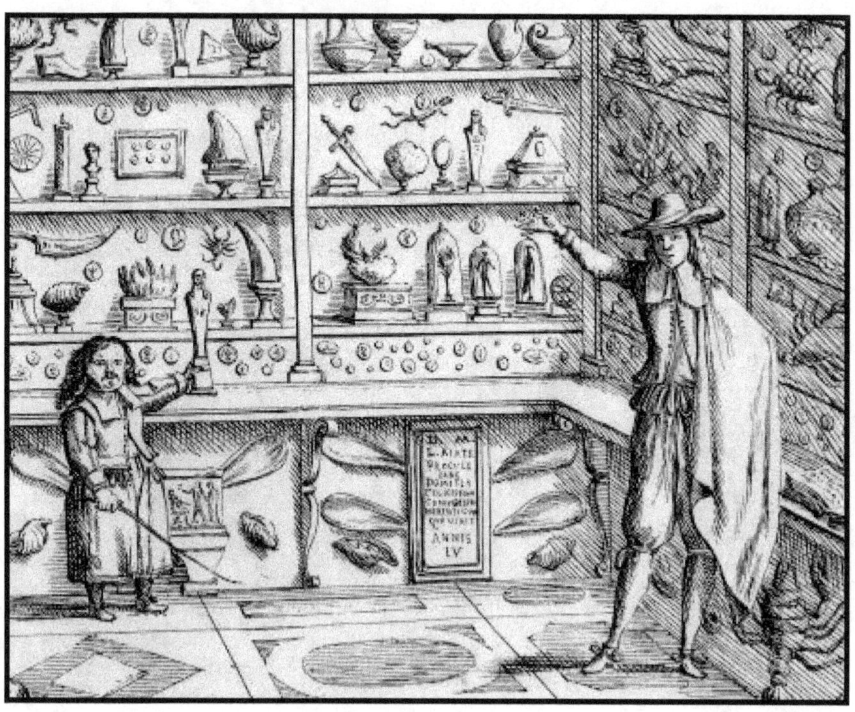

Fernando Cospi's personal museum, 1677

Introduction

Personal museums are a woefully underutilized medium for personal creative expression. One of the Zymoglyphic Museum's goals is to facilitate the creation of such mini-museums, so our education department has taken it upon itself to compile this handy guide to creating your own museum.

Our approach takes its inspiration from the curiosity cabinets, popular at the dawn of Europe's age of discovery. These early museums were more noted for their variety than for being scientific or educational, and showcased rare and wondrous objects.

Many people once had childhood museums, or created little scenes in the woods, or are driven to collect sticks, rusted objects, gnarled roots, flea market oddities, skulls, beach finds, or general detritus. The conceptual framework of a museum can be a useful way of bringing some sort of organization and significance such an accumulation.

 In a personal museum, these objects become souvenirs of trips to the far realms of the curator's consciousness. They may suggest a story or they may simply be interesting on their own, either as single objects or as interesting juxtapositions.

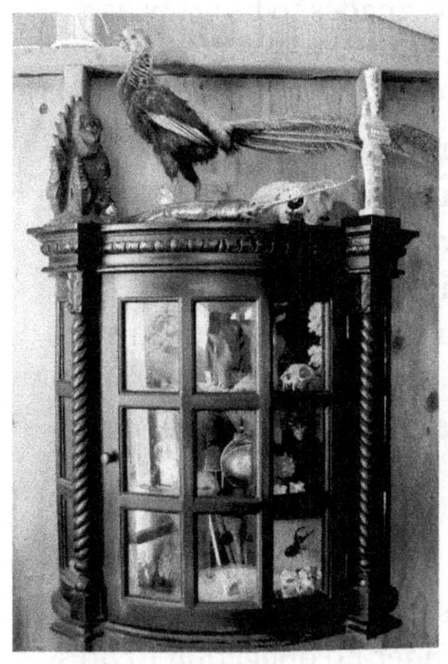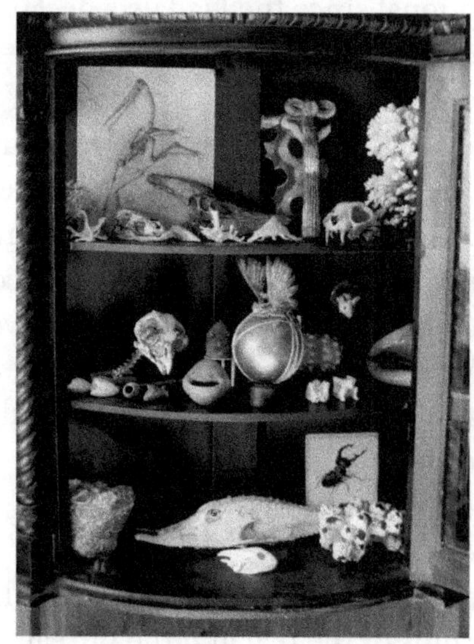

An eclectic collection of objects displayed in the style of a 17th century curiosity cabinet

Basic principles

The collection

A museum is ideally a collection of wondrous objects, arranged and presented in such a way as to intrigue, mystify, amaze, educate, or otherwise entrance the visitor. In a personal museum, the objects need not be valuable, rare, or historically important; they just need to express an important part of you, possibly in ways you are unable to explain. Ideally, when you are in your museum, it will feel like an externalized version of what's inside you.

Creator or curator?

A personal museum can be a mix of objects that you have made and objects you have collected—you can have a dual role as creator and curator. As a creator, the museum approach encourages variety in what your create. You can assign creatorship of what you make to yourself or to imaginary entities.

Is it art?

Art is a combination of craft, concept, and personal expression. Anyone can make art—there is a craft element, but it has been optional since the Dadaists declared readymades to be art over a hundred years ago. The goal here is an amalgam of objects that becomes a personal expression. If you wish, you may present the museum as conceptual, performance, or installation art.
If calling it "art" inhibits you for fear you will be judged on composition, artistic value, or some arcane criteria that you are not privy to, then don't call it art; just do what you feel like doing. It's a hobby, if you need a word. However, as Marshall McLuhan said, "Art is anything you can get away with." You can justify anything by calling it art. If you want some odd object, you can always say, "I need it for an art project."

Is it real?

A personal museum can have each of its metaphorical feet in the realms of the real and the unreal. It is under no obligation to present its findings and research as being literally true. You may choose to make your visitors wonder what is true or not. The Museum of Jurassic Technology, for example, specializes in this approach.

Will it be profitable?

Art is not generally a viable economic proposition—supply exceeds demand—so it makes more sense to do what you find satisfying and not let salability affect it. A museum approach is more amenable to showing your work than to selling it. There are ways in which a museum can bring in cash, such as charging admission, getting donations as a nonprofit organization, or selling souvenirs in a museum shop, but primarily museums are subsidized by public funds and/or wealthy benefactors. Your museum will likely be subsidized from your personal funds unless you can find a wealthy and willing patron. Attempts at monetization in any case should not be allowed to distort your personal vision of what the museum should be.

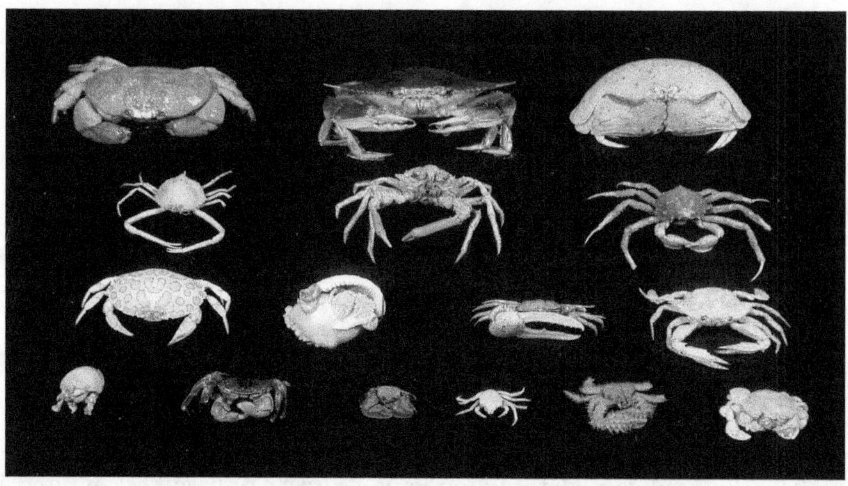

A collection of crabs illustrating natural variations on a theme

Things to do

Collect

Pick up or purchase objects that speak to you in some way. These objects may be found at thrift stores or garage sales, or they may be souvenirs of events or places you've been to, artifacts of personal importance, or beach finds. Pick some ordinary objects that stand out in some way from the background. You don't need to know or explain why.

Frame objects and collections

Objects take on significance when framed. A worn sea object (right) becomes an object of contemplation when oriented just so and placed on a pedestal; a simple collection of crabs (previous page) shows the wondrous variety in a related group of animals.

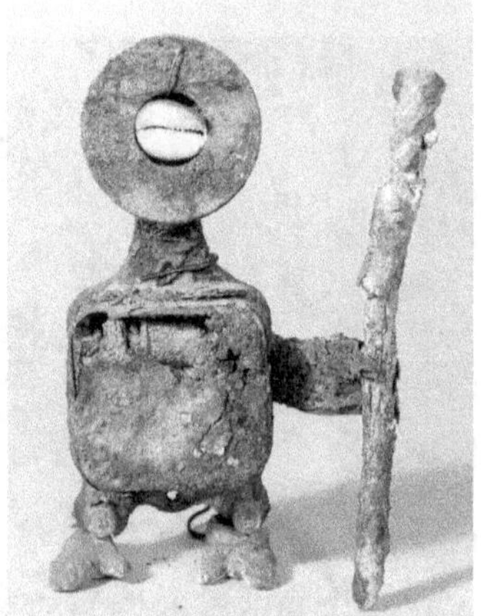

Make artifacts

In collecting, you are primarily relying on the inherent "interestingness" of objects, rather than making something yourself, but there are easy ways to create artifacts as well. For example, assemblages can be made from the objects you collect. Ideally, you will have an exhibit preparation area where you can spread out your finds and see what goes with what. As with collecting, you don't need to articulate the rationale for what you make—that will come later when you develop a theme and narrative.

Be spontaneous—just try making things with no preconceived notions and see what happens. A certain arrangement may take on a sort of glow of significance; it may be much later before you realize what the actual significance of the arrangement is.

A "Rust Age" artifact made from a rusty doorbell, a rusty washer, a cowry shell, and a large, barnacle-encrusted nail

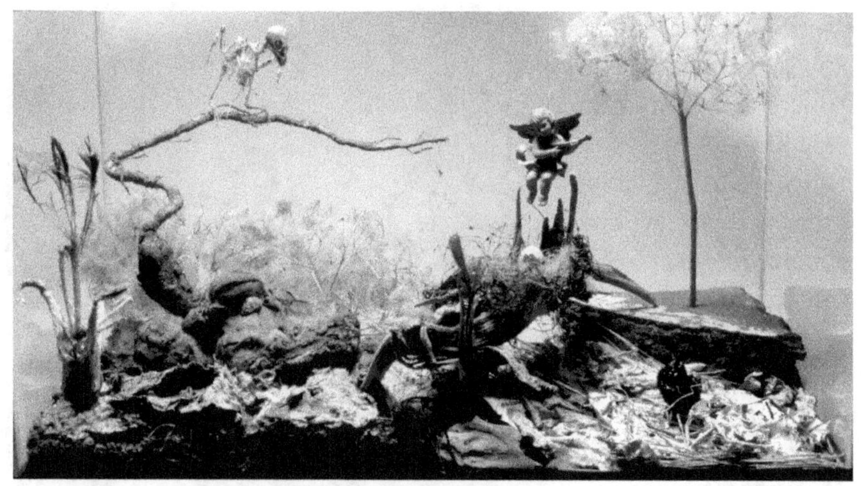

A small diorama constructed from an angel Christmas ornament, a piece of roadway, a discarded candy wrapper, bones, leaves, dirt, and other natural objects, all in a 10-gallon aquarium tank

Create dioramas

Dioramas are special type of display, an illustration of a scene, a narrative moment frozen in time. They can be constructed in 10-gallon aquarium tanks, which are generally cheap and come with built-in lighting. Alternatively, you can construct custom vitrines out of sheets of clear acrylic. After a diorama is completed, you can fill in the narrative and add explanatory signage. Dioramas may have either a terrestrial or a dry-aquarium theme. If you are a painter, you can incorporate backdrops for your scenes, or simply paint the glass black on three sides to make a visual enclosure. Scenes themselves may be constructed from papier-mâché or other techniques, or simply made just of natural materials (a bed of soil, sand, or moss). Model railroad literature has lots of tips on how to create convincing miniature landscapes.

Build the museum

The possibilities of the museum building are limited only by your means and available space. If you ever harbored dreams of being an architect, this is your chance to design and build an ideal edifice. Or you can simply acquire one—the Zymoglyphic Museum, for example, was once housed in an 8x12 prefabricated shed that was delivered and set up in a day.

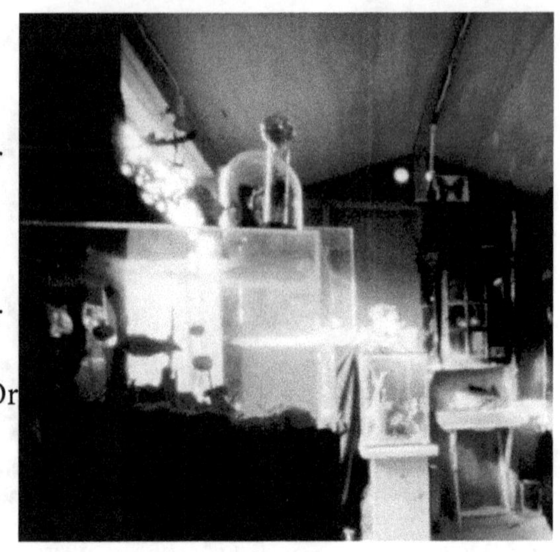

The interior of the Zymoglyphic Museum as seen through a pinhole camera

The Museum of Unnatural Selection was created out of a shipping container. You may devote a room in your house to your museum, or even convert a dollhouse to be a museum. The Zymoglyphic Museum has had miniature works mounted on pedestals and installed in a series of shoeboxes.

There are two basic types of display strategies, and you can use a mix of both. Specimens and artifacts may be neatly organized and accurately labeled, as in a modern museum, or displayed as jumble of widely disparate items whose cumulative effect is wonder rather than education. The latter approach was popular in the early days of Wunderkammern.

Objects take on air of significance if they are displayed in vitrines or bell jars and/or on pedestals or in a display case. Cases, shelving, and vitrines may be constructed or purchased, depending on your carpentry skills and interests. Signage may be ornate or simple, cryptic or clear.

Most museums have more holdings than have room to display them. If this becomes true in your case, you can have rotating exhibits.

Create themes and narratives

In the course of your collecting, making artifacts, and creating dioramas, look for themes that you can articulate or build on. Some tips:

- Perhaps you had collections or a little museum when you were a child, or made scenes in the woods—tap into that for your current museum theme.
- Let the objects that are close together suggest a compelling combination
- Mix the scientific and the fantastic
- Create artifacts of an imaginary civilization

Document the collections

Taking pictures of your objects can be a creative project in itself. Well-photographed objects can look more interesting in the photograph than they do in real life. Taking photographs of dioramas presents its own challenges! Pinhole photography, for example, in particular works well with dioramas due to its great depth of field. If you are not inclined toward photography as a medium of expression, encourage others to take photographs in your museum. Museums are very interesting environments for photographers and their interpretations may surprise you.

Document the museum

Many museums have guidebooks, often subtitled "A guide to the collections". These make excellent souvenirs for visitors to take home for reference. They are also an opportunity to showcase your photographs if that is an area of interest, or to expound on the founding principles and themes of your museum, or write up any narratives that are too long for your museum signage.

Create a persona

At a minimum, your role is the curator or director of the museum. You may want to flesh out the persona by taking on an imaginary alter-ego. For example, for his Wonders of the World Museum, Clayton Bailey became Professor Gladstone.

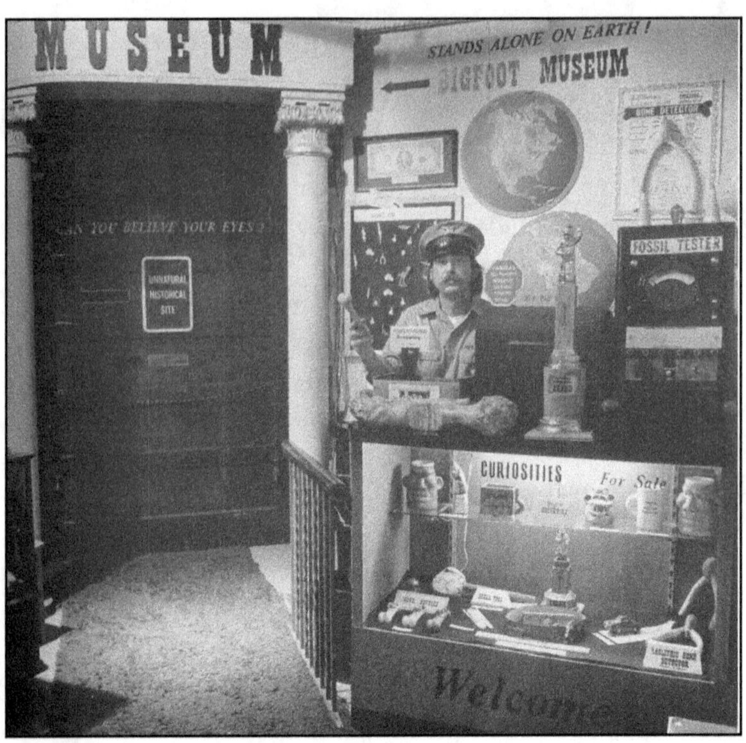

Clayton Bailey in persona as Dr. Gladstone in his Kaolithic Wonders of the World Museum, 1976

Outreach

Visitors

Once the museum is complete, it could become a private sanctuary for contemplation, since the museum will be like being inside your own subconscious mind. Most likely, though, you will want to have visitors. You can be open regularly or occasionally depending on your tolerance for talking to strangers. This is a good way to meet like-minded people, although you will get your share of curiosity-seekers as well. You may end up on lists of "quirky things to do" lists for your town. If you like this angle, you can get listed on Atlas Obscura for national and international exposure.

If you see your museum as an art project, being a "place to visit" means that your art will be exposed to people who would never go to an art gallery.

A Web site

Having a web site makes it possible to for people unable to visit your museum to know something about it. While not the same as visiting, it is better than nothing and may lead to interesting correspondence with like-minded people. A web site also enables you to link to like-minded sites who may well return the favor. You can also have an online version of the museum shop and online exhibits related to your theme.

A Web site is a good creative opportunity if you are interested in learning web technologies, graphic design or user interface design. The details of how to set up a web site are beyond the scope of this book, but here are some recommended design goals

* Keep it simple: have thumbnails to let visitors choose what looks interesting, and don't let the web design distract the focus away from your content

* Consider a fictional front end—a visitor may cruise around the site without ever really knowing what's going on, or they can look at an "About" page to get the real story.

* The site may be ever-evolving, but it should always appear complete at any given time (no "under construction" areas)

* Support random navigation. Most users will enter the site on an arbitrary page due to a search, rather than coming in through the front page

A blog

Maintaining a blog has many uses:

* Notification of events at the museum. Potential visitors can subscribe to your blog so that you need not update it frequently, if blogging is not your main task. At a minimum you will want to announce when the museum will be open.

* Share background and details about selected objects and exhibits

* Showcase writing and/or photography if desired—A nice format for a blog is a good picture accompanied by short, well-written text, with links for further reading,

* Links to like minded people. As of this writing, blogs seem

to be more popular than web sites for connectivity and there is more cross-linking than with web sites

• Promote other artists and institutions with a compatible mindset, especially those with little or no internet presence

The museum shop

Museum collections are not for sale, but museums generally provide gift shops that have items for sale. Large museums do this to make money, but it is unlikely that a personal museum's shop will, so think of it as a promotional enterprise. You can design t-shirts, or other souvenir items that visitors can take home as souvenirs of their visit. Companies such as Cafe Press and Zazzle will make limited run of objects with your designs. You can also sell your guidebook and any other books, pamphlets, or zines related to your museum theme.

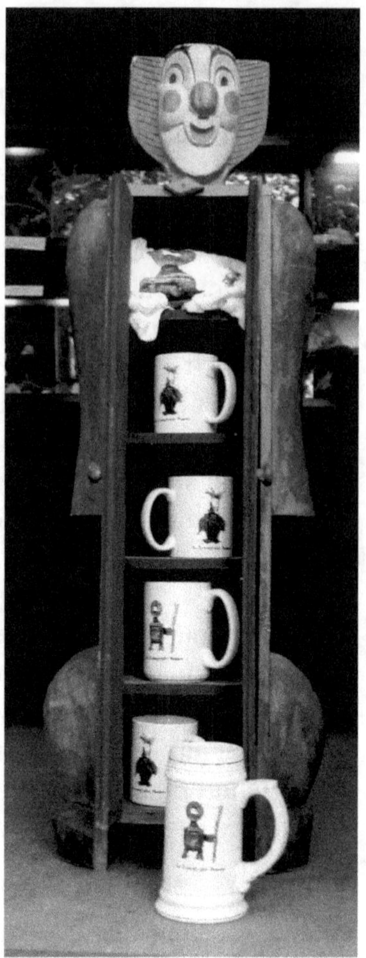

Zymoglyphic drinkware and t-shirts

Promotional materials

• Have business cards with a picture and the museum's URL available in your wallet, should the topic of "what do you do" come up in any social context.

• Consider having a brochure available at the museum so visitors can have something tangible to bring home and possibly reference later. This is an opportunity to boil down your vision of the museum to its essence and present it succinctly in words and pictures.

• Since you are a place being visited, you can offer postcards for people to keep as miniature art or to send to friends and relatives.

Get other people involved

The institutional identity of your museum means that there are predefined roles that others can play in your museum

  • Interns and volunteers—people who help out with various tasks while learning about what your museum does for the community

  • Donors—Once your museum is established, you will probably find people wanting to donate items to it, often items that they themselves have collected but do not have a proper context for. You may wish to acquire these objects or encourage the donors to set up their own museums.

In Conclusion

The Zymoglyphic Museum would be most interested in hearing about any projects resulting from or inspired by this pamphlet!
Contact the museum at zymoglyphic@gmail.com

Books for reference
Arany, Lynn and Archie Hobson *Little Museums: Over 1,000 Small (and Not-So-Small) American Showplaces*
Brown, Vinson *Building your own Nature Museum*
Mauries, Patrick *Cabinets of Curiosities*
Neal, Arminta *Exhibits for the Small Museum*
Putnam, James *Art and Artifact: The Museum as Medium*

Photo Credits
All photos by the author except as follows:
Photos on p. 7 by Judith Hoffman
Photo on p. 9 used by permission of Clayton Bailey

Published by the Zymoglyphic Museum Press
© 2015 Jim Stewart

ORBITAL VIEWS

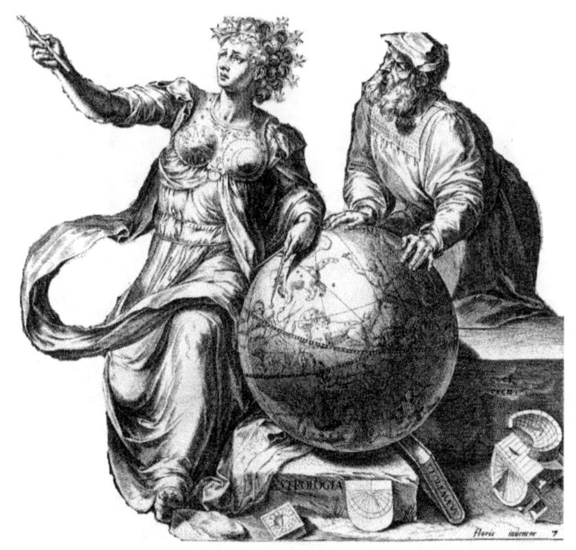

The Zymoglyphic Museum: Semiotics of a Fictocryptic Portland Institution

Stanislaw Strzybisz (The Fictocryptic Institute)[1]

Reprinted from The Proceedings of the Society for Esoteric Museology, *July 2017*

ABSTRACT

The Zymoglyphic Museum is an enigmatic institution whose purpose and mission remain obscure despite diligent efforts on the part of researchers to weave its many loose threads of meaning into some coherent framework. The author here presents an overview of the museum as physically constituted, then undertakes a novel interrogative-analytical approach to excavating the essence of the museum from its many layers of metaphysical cruft, culminating in an analysis of the key question, "What does 'zymoglyphic' mean?".

BACKGROUND

The Zymoglyphic Museum is sited at the base of an extinct urban volcano in a bucolic neighborhood of Portland, Oregon, colloquially known as "Tabor Holler". The museum outwardly resembles nothing so much as a carriage house or freestanding garage with a second story added atop. A modest sign on the door identifies the museum and lists the few hours that it is open to the public. An enormous douglas-fir tree looms over it.

---

[1] Stanislaw Strzybisz is the founder and principal of the Fictocryptic Institute, an anonymously funded think tank whose mission is the study of organizations and organisms that exist in the realm between the possible, the probable, and the imaginary.

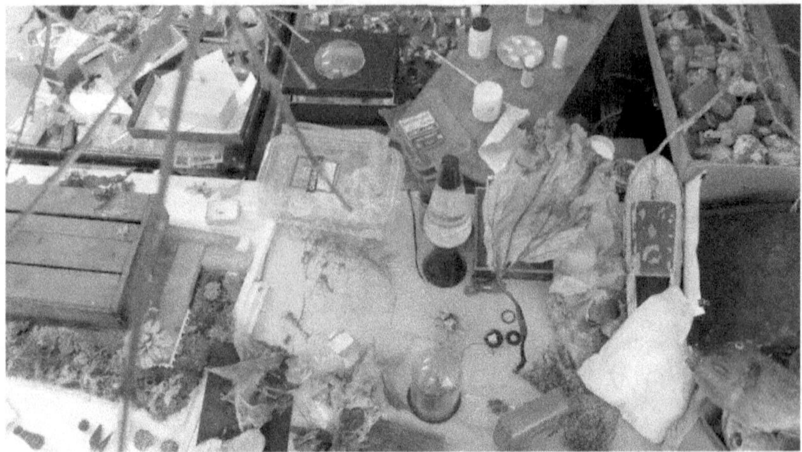

Fig. 1: Exhibit preparation area

THE EXHIBITS

Upon entering the museum, visitors are directed (sometimes ushered) past the chaotic exhibit preparation area that comprises most of the first floor *[Fig. 1]*, through a small stairwell gallery and up the staircase to the exhibit halls. The first exhibits encountered, near the top of the stairs, are collections of specimens from the natural world—a small mineral cabinet[2] an array of picture rocks (presented as a miniature art gallery), a crab collection, shadowboxes with rows of neatly pinned insects, and the museum's signature collection of Xenophora (sea snails that collect objects and are billed as "Assemblage Artists of the Deep")[3] *[Fig. 2]*.

The east wall of the museum ushers us into the Rust Age of the Zymoglyphic region. Here, we are introduced to the ancient culture for which the museum is named. These excavated and reconstructed artifacts range from "primitive" pieces such as "Guardian Figure" *[Fig.3]*, "Shamanic Figure", and "Wooden Mask" (presumed to have been used in various spiritual practices) to more functional items such as bioluminescent fungus

---

2 "In large calm halls, a stately Museum shall teach you the infinite, solemn lessons of Minerals" Whitman, W. *Leaves of Grass* 1871

3 Giaimo, Cara "Up Close and Personal With the World's Most Artistic Mollusks: Deep sea 'carrier snails' painstakingly turn their shells into tiny dioramas." Atlas Obscura, April 18, 2017

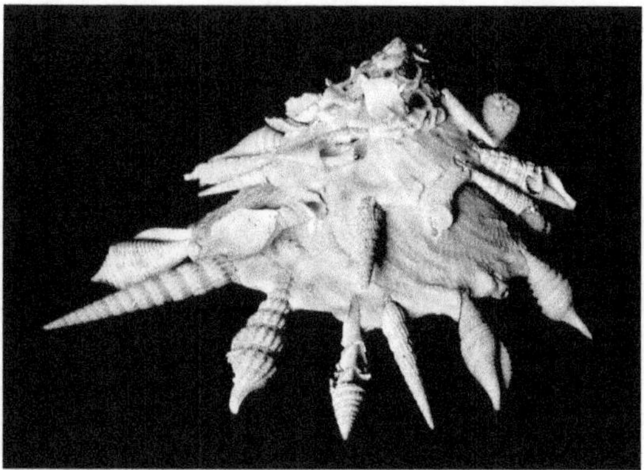

Fig. 2: *Xenophora pallidula*, from the museum's Xenophora collection

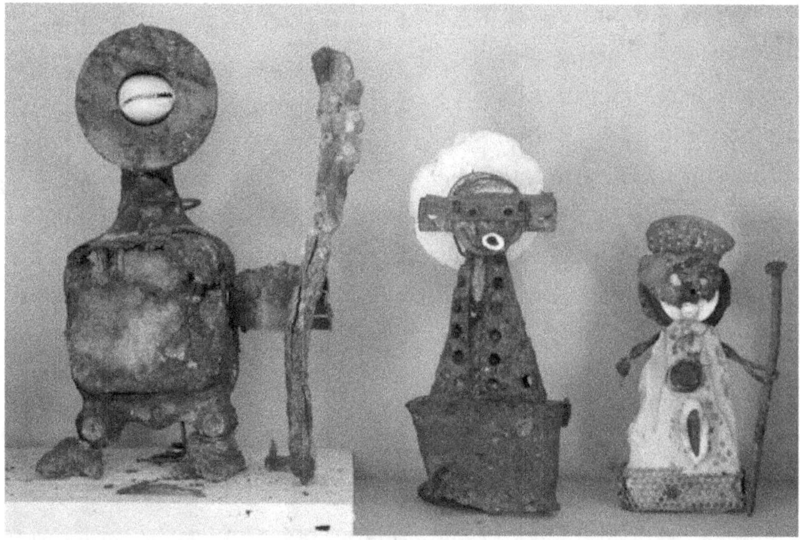

Fig. 3: Rust Age figurines, including Guardian Figure (left)

lamps and pre-literate books. As this was a pre-literate culture, the actual meaning of these objects is speculative at best and based on similar cultures that have survived into the modern age. However, even divorced from any original spiritual function and mounted trophy-like on the wall of a museum, these artifacts retain a fascination based on their aesthetics alone.

Continuing clockwise around the main exhibit hall, we enter the Age of Wonder. This area has won the museum a reputation as being itself a "wunderkammer" in the Renaissance tradition[4]; this belief in turn has led some to believe that the museum is simply a collection of oddities in the tradition of Ripley or Barnum. One display, the wall-mounted curiosity cabinet *[Fig. 4]*, has clear parallels to Europe's so-called Age of Exploration, with its fascination with newly discovered, fanciful creatures, and artifacts from exotic cultures.

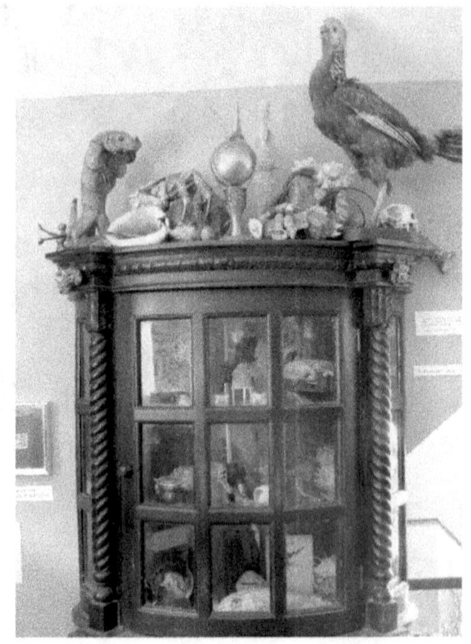

Fig. 4: Wall-mounted curiosity cabinet

In addition to representative artifacts from the Age of Wonder (a strange alchemy apparatus crude orrery, various memento mori[5], miniature grottoes, etc.) there are a number of enigmatic poster-size illustrations purporting to showcase life in the Zymoglyphic region during this period, the imagery apparently cobbled together from alchemical, allegorical and other sources.

The Age of Wonder hall includes a number of dioramas, large and small, containing natural objects and figures arranged with some narrative theme. The smallest ones, contained in ten-gallon fish tanks, resemble dessicated terraria and aquaria, often giving the impression that some living creature may yet survive in them. Two larger dioramas

---

[4] "...a goodly huge Cabinet, wherein whatsoever the Hand of Man by Art or Engine has made rare in Stuff, Form or Motion; whatsoever Singularity, Chance, and the Shuffle of things hath produced, whatsoever Nature has wrought in things that want Life and may be kept, shall be sorted and included" Bacon, Sir Francis *Gesta Grayorum* 1594

[5] Memento mori were inspirational objects with skull, bone, and other death motifs intended to remind you of the inevitability of your ultimate demise and thus motivate you to make good use of your remaining hours.

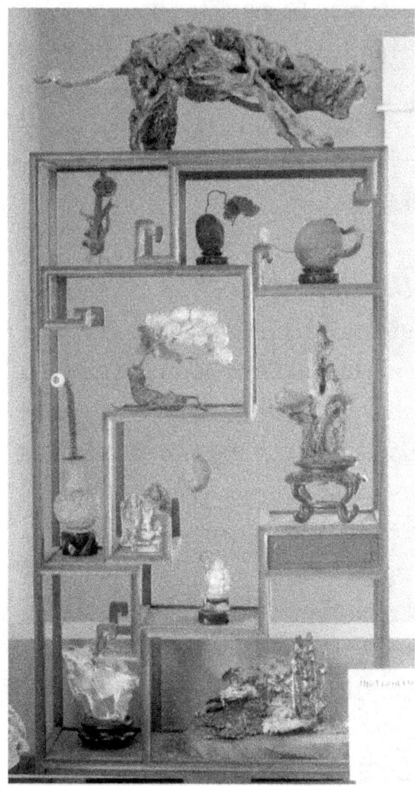

Fig. 5: Display typical of the Era of Oriental Influence

(estimated at 180 and 500 gallons respectively) are unenclosed and spill out somewhat into the visitor space. Unlike the natural history museums of our region, it seems there was no requirement for the narratives in these scenes to be a literal recreation of events in the natural world, only that they primarily consist of natural objects. This combination gives them a dreamy, mythical air while consisting of undeniably material, often ordinary, components.

Around the corner from the dioramas we find the Era of Oriental Influence exhibit. According to the label, Zymoglyphic explorers during the Age of Wonder made contact with a culture whose aesthetic was immediately seized upon. Overly elaborate art works fell out of fashion in the region, and in their stead appeared small, quiet, serene works made for contemplation, perhaps a simple tray landscape or a gnarled rock or stick mounted on a stand. They were generally displayed in special shelving *[Fig. 5]*.

The final portion of the tour brings up to The Modern Age, showcasing the latest technological advances in Zymoglyphic aesthetics. The futuristic exhibit "The Aquarium of Tomorrow" is a cybernetic wonder that generates a hypnotic, never-repeating virtual aquarium from such basic elements as pixels, lines, circles, color, motion, chance, algorithms, and feedback loops. On another screen, the "views" from the Age of Wonder have been animated into a sort of wordless documentary. As modern times continue, more exhibits may be expected here.

We now find that we have come full circle and are back where we started. The future of exhibit development seems to be linking the modern age with the far past, all the way back to the Mud Age, attempting a laboratory recreation of the primordial ooze in silicon- and hydrocarbon- based life forms.

THE MUSEUM'S SOCIAL AND CULTURAL CONTEXT

The museum has an ambiguous relationship to the Portland community. The curator, sometimes glimpsed scurrying in the shadows, is rumored to be a Silicon Valley refugee and thus considered an invasive species by some Portland residents. Others welcome the museum as a worthy successor to such no longer extant Portland institutions as the Faux Museum and the Bathtub Art Museum. A local "alternative-weekly" periodical recently included the museum in its "Best of Portland" issue only six months into the museum's operation.[6]

Museum logs tally 591 visitors to the museum in its first seven months of operation (January through July of 2017). Average attendance is 35.9 per open day, with a range from fourteen to sixty-four. Time spent by visitors in the museum area ranges from ten minutes or so (presumably those for whom the museum was not what they were led to expect) to well over an hour (often a patron intent on comprehensive photographic documentation).

Visitors to the museum primarily divide into two groups: those for whom the museum is a prime exemplar of "quirky Portland" (these further divide into out-of-town-visitors who have heard about the museum[7] and locals who are either new to the area or have a visitor in tow) and a more select group comprised of those who have similar tastes and are pleased to find that they are, and perhaps always have been, zymoglyphiles. These latter, if local and sufficiently enthusiastic, are

---

[6] Korfhage, Matthew "Best Rogue Taxidermist" *Willamette Week*, June 12, 2017.

[7] Visitors primarily learn of the museum through the popular off-beat-travel Web site *Atlas Obscura*

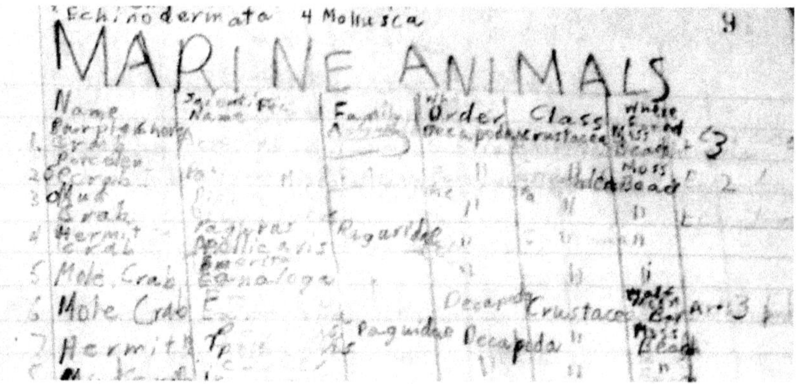

Fig. 6: Page from original museum catalog, 1960

rumored to be recruited by the curator into a shadowy organization or cult for acolytes of the Zymoglyphic Way.

INTERROGATIVE ANALYSIS

Certain questions come up repeatedly as visitors interact with the curator, and examining them is key to determining community expectations of the museum and thus an indicator of what the museum means to the community. No records have been kept of exact number of times a given question has been asked, but there is a short list of frequent interrogatives.

"How long have you been doing this?"
As the roots of the museum date back nearly a half-century this question can have a very long answer. The museum is at heart a vastly expanded and metastasized version of the curator's (unnamed and very literal) childhood museum of rocks, shells, arrowheads, marine animals, insects, and bits of history[8], adding an aesthetic overlay, presenting natural creations as art objects, and expanding into other media.

"Did you make all of this?"

[8] Stewart, Jim "Science Notebook and Catalog", MS 1960 See Fig. 6

People are often as concerned with the provenance objects in a museum as with its immediately apparent aesthetic properties. This question helps to distinguish the museum as a proper museum (a themed collection of objects from various sources) from a "museum" (possibly an art installation to be credited to a specific person).

"What's your favorite piece?"
This is thought to be a question that deflects attention from the patron's response to the museum onto to the curator's intention. The curator's standard answer deflects back, something along the lines of "I see it as all one unified work so I can't pick out any favorites."

"Do you sell your work or is this just a hobby?"
This question of course presupposes that art must have a monetary value in order to be taken seriously, or that the artist must make art-making a career in order to be taken seriously.

"What IS that thing?"
Many objects in the museum, like the museum itself, are ambiguous in nature. Natural objects placed in a novel context, a scene in diorama for example, may become unrecognizable.

"What does 'zymoglyphic' mean?"
This deceptively simple but deeply semiotic question is at very heart of any zymoglyphological analysis worthy of the name. It is invariably the first one formed on the lips of a novice or unprepared visitor to the museum. A formal definition of the word is posted in two places in the museum as well as on the museum's Web site *[Fig. 7]*, but even after reading it, and visiting the museum, one may well wonder exactly what makes a given object, collection, idea, or environment truly "zymoglyphic".

Zymoglyphologists and related scholars have debated the deeper meaning of the word for a long time. One researcher's empirical approach posited that anything included in the museum was by defini-

> **zy'-mo-glyph'-ic**, adj. [Gr. *zyme* leaven + Gr. *glyphe* carving]
> 1. Of, or pertaining to, images of fermentation, specifically the solid residue of creative fermentation on natural objects
> 2. The collection and arrangement of objects, primarily either natural or weathered by natural forces, for poetic effect

Fig. 7: Sign with formal definition of the term "zymoglyphic"

tion zymoglyphic and proposed a taxonomy of the museum's exhibits, holdings, and other entities[9].

- Specimen collections (pure naturalia, similar to a natural history museum)
- Natural objects collected and recontextualized as art objects
- Slightly modified natural objects (usually adding an eye or two, or placing miniature figures on an object to make a landscape
- Assemblages of natural objects and/or decayed metal, with or without backstory
- Curiosity cabinets (jumbled collections of naturalia and artificialia, including anonymous art made by others ("folk art", indigenous art) and art by known artists

This attempt was ultimately abandoned in the face of an unceasingly bewildering array of media still to be dealt with (postage stamps, animation, computer programs, abstract paintings and so on) and the further complication that entities can be contained within other entities, thus requiring a hierarchical, if not downright fractal, taxonomic design. With the usual hackneyed plea for "further investigation", these researchers threw a gauntlet down which has yet to be taken up.

In fact, every part of the museum, from the whole down to the indi-

[9] Strzybisz, S. "Taxonomy of objects in the Zymoglyphic Museum" Proceedings of the Society for Esoteric Museology, January, 2016

vidual objects and components, seems to exist in an indeterminate state of not falling into one category or another. It is not strictly speaking a literal museum or an installation art piece. Individual pieces often rely on parts that seem to be one thing but are in fact something else. One could claim that, as with quantum mechanics, the ambiguity does not resolve until there is an observer to make it happen.

A related question is "Is it art?" Are parts of it art and parts not? Is a crab collection art? Does a non-art object become art by being placed within an art context? Are the items available in the museum shop, such as postcards, art? Is the whole thing a single, integrated, work of art as the curator implies? Does it matter? The museum and its curator seem to have no art world connections in the way of credentials or gallery affiliation, the sole exception being an essay written by a noted Los Angeles art critic in which he defends the museum's claim that "nature can make art".[10]

Others have argued that the museum is akin to a living organism and that any part of it ceases to have life once removed from the context of the museum.

A more fruitful approach may be a parallel to the Surrealist search for the marvelous, defined as follows: "a state of extreme poetic tension at which inner and outer realities are joined and the individual is simultaneously one with himself and the world, thus recovering the true sense of the sacred"[11]

Ultimately, there does not appear to be a quantifiable answer to the question of what "zymoglyphic" means. Empirical approaches break down due to the inherent ambiguity of the subject, and deductive approaches are similarly stymied. Each new approach brings more questions than answers. A gauntlet is hereby thrown.

---

[10] Frank, Peter "The Art World Beneath our Feet: *The Zymoglyphic Museum and its Mission*" in Stewart, Jim The Zymoglyphic Museum: A Guide to the Collections, 2nd edition, 2010

[11] "Mabile, Pierre *Mirror of the Marvelous* 1962"

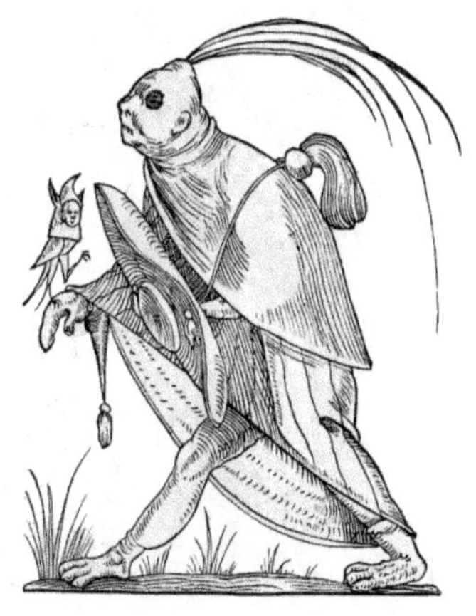

Stanislaw Strzybisz is the founder and principal of the Fictocryptic Institute. He was the product of the curator's longing to have a scholarly article written about the museum. This article was originally published in *Portland 2017: An Anthology* (Shannon St. Hilaire et al, eds., 2018).

The Art World Beneath our Feet: The Zymoglyphic Museum and its Mission

Peter Frank

Since about the time some homo sapiens, or reasonable facsimiles thereof, first rendered images on the walls of a cave[1], said species has regarded itself as distinct from – above – nature. Sure, has gone the thinking, nature is a creative force, maybe bigger and fiercer than we'll ever be, but in its very elementality it is not an artistic force, y'know, the way we are. In other words, nature makes the world, we make art. Not so fast. We make the world, too – for better or worse. The whole ecological movement places responsibility for the recent, increasingly drastic changes in the natural order at our feet. We have a demonstrable impact upon the natural order, locally and (increasingly) globally, as do no other sentient beings. Therefore, it would stand to reason that, if we can make the world (even though we can't seem to make it to our liking)[2], nature can make art.

Look at it another way. "Art," at least as much as beauty, is in the eye of the beholder. It is a matter of perception, a condition of discourse, not an inherent quality. If someone sees something as art, it's art. If someone says something is art, it's art. That doesn't make it good, worthwhile, or an embodiment of truth or morality. Designating something as art doesn't let it off the hook. Art can be inhumane, reprehensible, evil, and still be art.[3] And, in this regard, art can be entirely amoral, sourced in non-sentient forces beyond even the social impulses of, oh, creatures of air and sea. Neither fish nor fowl can see "art," and don't need or care to. But we see their coloration, their shapes, their sounds as art. Scientists band such creatures; perhaps artists should sign them.[4]

All this is proffered in defense of – no, actually, as explanation for – the philosophy underlying the Zymoglyphic Museum and the realm of art and inquest it serves to repose. The objects collected by and into the Museum have relied as much on the intervention of nature for their existence and identity as on the intervention of humans, perhaps more so. They are organically produced or naturally modified. Of course, they are naturally produced, as are we all.[5] But they escape the norms of natural production in falling through nature's cracks, as it were, having been subjected to metamorphic forces which have degraded or otherwise transformed them into forms and presences we tend, in context, to regard as unusual – unusual not simply in their appearance, but in their "artful" effect upon us. Or do we, in regarding them as art, have an artful effect on them? This conundrum of appearances – nature just does its thing, we come along and designate various of its caprices "art," and all of a sudden nature is the ultimate artist – drives the Zymoglyphic Museum and indeed the whole Zymoglyphic ethos.

Yes, there is a Zymoglyphic ethos. There needs to be. Where otherwise would art end and nature begin? Or, rather, how would we otherwise explain the fact that nature doesn't seem to leave off where art begins (and vice versa)? Yes, it is an ethos, transcending (while not abandoning) aesthetics, encompassing human impulses and needs. It feeds on itself, self-evidently, narrowing the ethical argument down to one of aesthetics after all – but that in itself comprises an ethical argument, or, more to the point, a demonstration of an ethically charged condition. Is it right to artify nature?[6] Is this some kind of attempt to colonize the natural world, to insist that it once again "perform" for (the benefit of) humans?

The delights provided us by the Zymoglyphic Museum's myriad selections, and even by the relatively elaborate annotations and codifications with which the Museum provides its holdings, are themselves self-evident. The poetry of form, lyricism of association, and economy of function that define every concatenation, that pervade every diorama, rivet us to these apparitions, cementing our fascination and our affection. By inference, they cement our fascination and affection to nature itself. Perhaps that gilds the lily, so to speak. But, even in this era of ecological fetishism, perhaps not.[7]

The Zymoglyphic Museum itself did not spring fully blown from the hands and minds of ecological fetishists. Its contents were preceded on this earth by everything from tree architecture to the juxtapositional reveries of the surrealists. Indeed, the Museum's holdings would seem to reawaken many of Andre Breton's most profound and most capricious dicta,[8] and its two-dimensional features descend from the narrative collages of Max Ernst and the photomontages of his dada compeers. And, just as those collages and photomontages begat the ever more riotous and cinematic elaborations of Bruce Conner, Jordan Belson, Akbar del Piombo, Sätty, and a host of others, the surrealists' freestanding confabulations led to a burgeoning assemblage "movement" that may have crested in the early 1960s but has never truly abated.

The Zymoglyphic Museum is itself the latest – arguably ultimate – in a long cascade of gentle Wunderkammers. The modern "museum" indeed began as such a phenomenon, a trophy house of oddments compiled by a particularly vital-minded (or bored) nobleman. Refined, almost refracted, into the carefully collected, carefully crafted lesson in art and/or science we know as today's museum, the Wunderkammer still proposed a spirit of ravenous, unfettered adventure, whether one that roamed the globe or one that roamed the neighborhood. For instance, the Zymoglyphic Museum's most immediate predecessor, the famed, if short-lived, Fred Gallery, featured items isolated from an emphatically constricted region.[9]

Still and all, the Zymoglyphic Museum, not least in its dedication to the artfulness of the non-human spirit, distinguishes itself among centers devoted to the found and/or founded object. Such an object may or may not have been touched by human hands in its formulation; but it took Nature to formulate it in its essence, and it took humankind to call it "art." Is Fred itself, then, dead? No, but, thanks to Nature,[10] Art is still alive.

Los Angeles
September 2010

[1] Lascaux, say, or Altamira.

[2] Our supposed degradation of nature is in fact nothing more than a degradation of the nature that sustains us. When natural conditions become inhospitable, they will still be natural conditions.

[3] Karlheinz Stockhausen declared the 9/11 attacks a work of art, acknowledging the craft of their perpetrators and recognizing in the attacks the experience of Kantian sublimity.

[4] Any number of artists have come close – Jannis Kounellis, for instance, exhibiting stabled horses in his gallery show, Piero Manzoni signing live nude women – but no one has applied Duchamp's concept of the Readymade directly to animals. Plants, perhaps, but not animals....

[5] As Jackson Pollock noted, "I am nature."

[6] There are, not surprisingly, many precedents. To name one, as reported by musicologist Nicolas Slonimsky, his "furfuraceous" friend, Fluxus artist Ken Friedman, claimed the March 1971 Sylmar earthquake as the last movement of his Third Symphony.

[7] Drill, baby, drill.

[8] In the early 1930s, to make the Expositions Surréalistes ever more provocative, Breton invited his surrealist minions to produce objects, especially

objects invented from other, already extant objects. This is precisely what Nature has done here (with a little help from its friends).

[9] The region consisted approximately of the streets around Columbia University In The City Of New York, not to mention the campus itself. It is no accident that at least one of the Zymoglyphic Museum's founders had a hand in founding and maintaining the closet-sized, world-shaking Gallery, dedicated, of course, to the proposition that "Art Is Dead, Long Live Fred."

[10] ...and, it goes without saying, the crew of experts comprising Team Zymoglyphic...

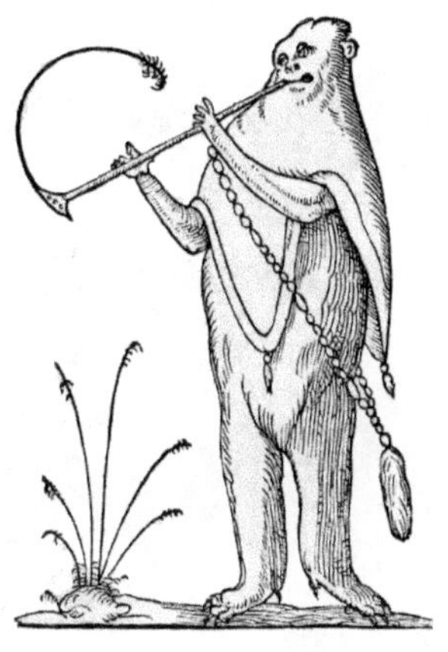

Peter Frank is a long-time L.A.-based art critic. He was senior curator of the Riverside Art Museum at the time of writing this article, which originally appeared as the foreword to the second edition of *The Zymoglyphic Museum: A Guide to the Collections* (2010)

The Artifice of Constructs in the Gilded Object: an Electroplating of Experience

Chandra Glaeseman

The Zymoglyphic Museum is an exercise in futility. It is a demonstration of the trans-dimensional space that is in constant flux in our waking and resting lives, never tethered to a singular platform except that of the individual experiencing. Life and death co-inhabit and the death of a being simply marks the space of departure of one energy and the beginning of a new one. Upon death, the life of decay takes over and negates the terminal point of presumption. Intentional activation of the found object breathes a new life, both in context and through simple recognition in an attempt to create spiritual zombies or resurrected saviors that bridge histories and offer meaning. They are shells of life until activated, offering space to the maker and to the viewer, as separate experiences, requesting that they (the objects) become a carrier that will facilitate a deeper understanding of the world around us. This funerary barge ushers the examination of the strangeness and the ordinariness of existences thereby creating a mythical and spiritual connection of the world and underworld.

Dust to dust; an extraction from the mortal coil

The contemporary funeral industry, one established at the turn of the 19th century, rearranged the peculiar customs of the disposal of the dead. Guilt has become gilded and sorrow capitalized upon by providing a salve of objects and opulence in an intentional misdirection of the idea of value. Expense of the dispensed has become indoctrinated and expected as affluence has been conflated with life worth. A simple shroud is no longer enough because it doesn't demonstrate the lavishness of the life it cloaked. Instead of looking toward and into other realms with humility to create spiritual passage, the gilded life of the recently deceased becomes so weighted down with artifice that it sinks and becomes buried deep into the substrata of fear. Symbolic language has created a lexicon of terminology intended to sanitize the experience of death. Undertakers are now funeral directors, coffins are caskets, hearses are coaches, cremated ashes are cremains and corpses are loved ones. The experience of death is orchestrated with such specificity that it has become a way of life replete with such depersonalization that detachment replaces mourning. The personal processes once venerated have been held at such distance that we are no longer performing a ritual that is our own. Instead, we allow the space of the sacred to become inhabited by the mechanization of the movements of those who handle death daily.

Museumification of objects and stories has also, up until very recently, sanitized history and supported the hierarchical standards of utility and worth in the world, while attempting to defeat the decomposition of articles of cultural importance. The precursors to museums, the cabinet of curiosities, emerged in the 16th century as vehicles to display exotic findings that described world travel and conquest as well as suggested a particularly affluent socioeconomic status. A distinction between education and entertainment cleaved into the 19th century museum that was fraught with snake oil and the artifice of theater creating an even deeper chasm between classes and access to knowledge. While ensconced with legitimate scientific inquiry, a certain elitism has followed the museum into the 21st century as not only the subject matter but the cost associated with visitation curbs accessibility. There is no doubt an awe that happens when being in the presence of antiquities and rare artifacts; a pleasure, a humility, a joy. And it is this experience that feeds the thirst for knowledge and stimulates the curiosity to keep going back, to keep exploring and to keep building context as the first person authors of our own existence.

Nitrous

The Zymoglyphic Museum, on the other hand, is an act of subversion. As a construct, it pokes at the idea of a museum as a cultural vault and rearranges the hierarchy of valuing the discarded object, a process not unlike the co-opting of the funeral industry, but with drastically different objectives.
The subversive act begins with collection in which the collector seemingly dons X-ray glasses that allow him to see what most don't or can't or won't. He notices the nooks and the crannies and the beauty of what nature has sloughed. Collection seems

compulsive. Like the bower bird dedicated to neatly arranging his abundance of unnecessaries, our collector gathers and cultivates object-poems to create a sculpted experience in vitrines and fish tanks and on plinths and pedestals.

Described as creative fermentation, found objects are intersected mid-decay and sent on a wild epistemological detour that rearranges a metaphorical composition resulting in an artifactual poetry. The once-dead object inflates with the effervescence of the collector turned director. With visual lyricism the object becomes buoyant, self-possessed and often times, silly. Humor is discovered in a space that is often reserved for solemnity as googly eyes are glued to carcasses and a turtle with a Tesla coil growing out of its back posit a new way of generating energy. Very serious in execution and borrowing from a taxonomic noesis, the presentation suggests a hint of tom-foolery that infuses benign objects with a spiraling energy catapulting it into a mythological space of fantastical narratives.

It is through these narratives, both curated and created, that our director invites his viewer to take part in the exploration of the internal and external world we all inhabit. As viewers, we dance between the paradoxical spaces of art versus non-art. We are neither pushed nor pulled in any one direction, but are instead invited to linger like a balloon in the breezy warehouse of the imagination, lilting towards dusty cabinets of logical hypotheses, ruminating in corridors of emotion and experience and breathing our own life into the cobwebs and pond scum that challenge mortality.

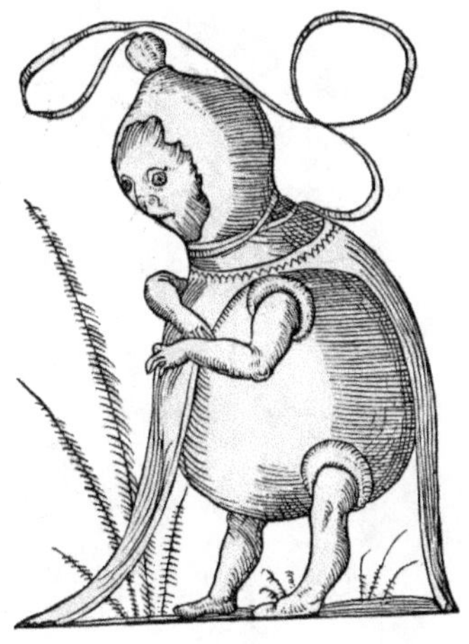

Chandra Glaeseman is a Portland-based visual artist and art educator, noted for her reuse of discarded materials. She was one of the original artists in the GLEAN residency, in which art is created from materials found at the local waste management facility. She is currently director of Portland Art and Learning Studios, a center for artists with intellectual and developmental disabilities.

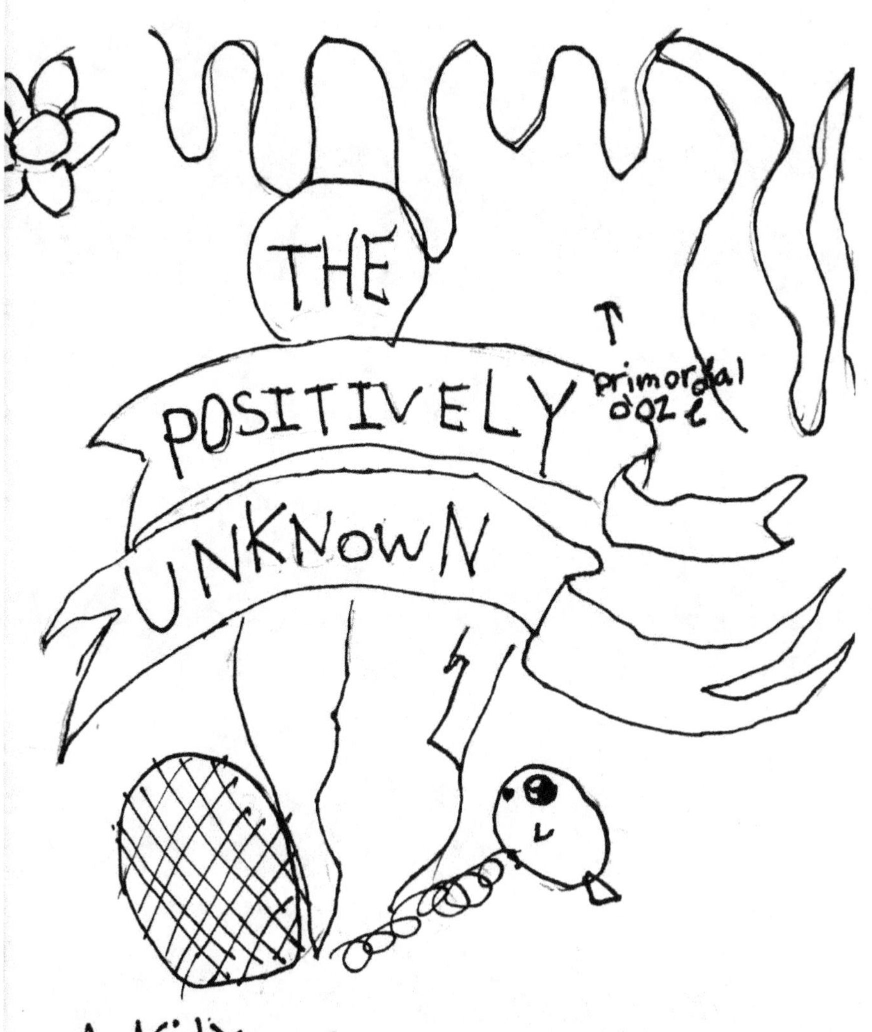

A Kid's Guide to the
Zymoglyphic Museum
By Alex Gaston

The positvely unknown: A kid's Glude to the Zymoglyphic musem.

By

((Alex Lily Gaston))

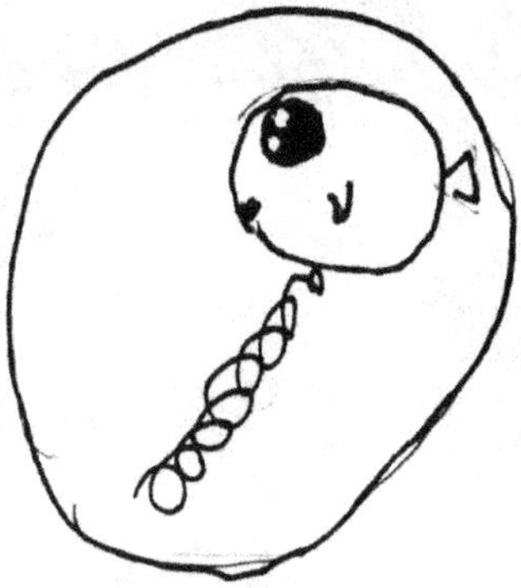

the Zymoglyphic Museum is owned and createated by Jim Stewart. thank you for making this magical world.

I like this hedgehog
Becuse it's cute! did you
know that there are 17
Species of hedgehogs! can you
find it?

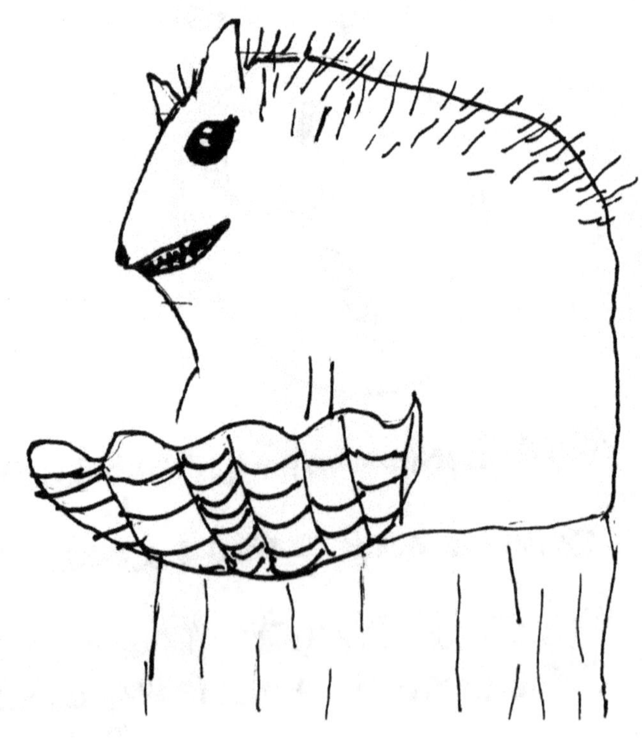

Its not scary, but I would recommend it for ages 6 and up!

the Eyeball carrot was created By Jim. the Eyeball carrot is very funny! have you went to the Zymoglyphic museum? I have. and Im planing on going loo more times! I think the Eyeball carrot is really good for kid becuse it is laughable.

This is a Tarantula molt (skin).
Tarantulas   shed   there skin
like snakes. Female tarantulas
Live Longer   than males.

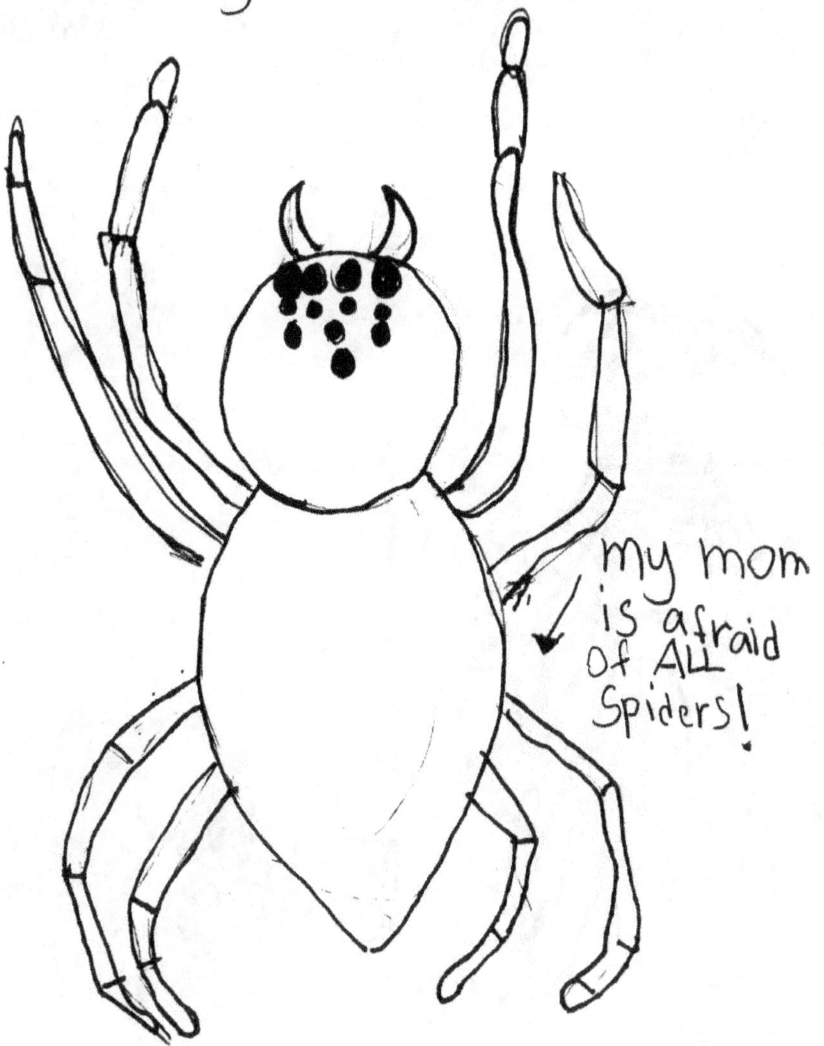

Moon Man with broken pot.
this moon Man has just landed
on the Zymoglyphic woird
and discovered a broken
pot.

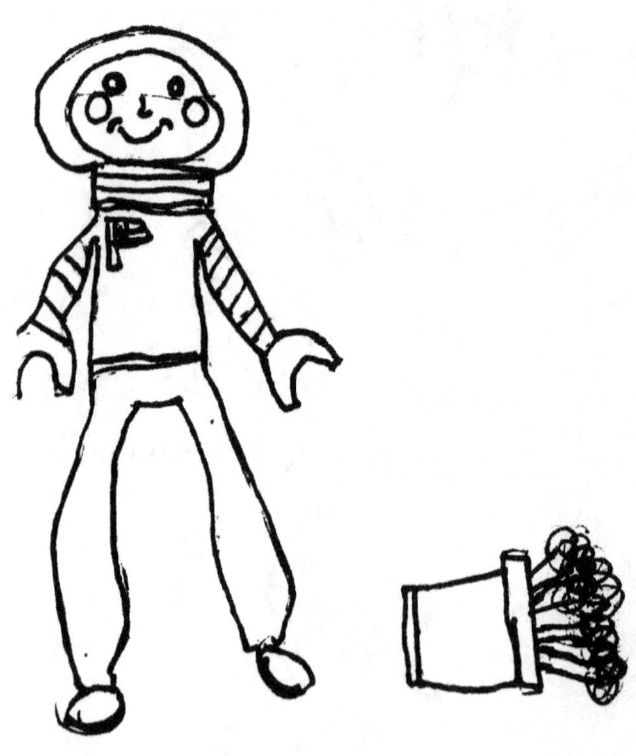

This is the Mermaid.
It is my favorite
Zymoglyphic. What ocean
do you think this
Mermaid lives in?

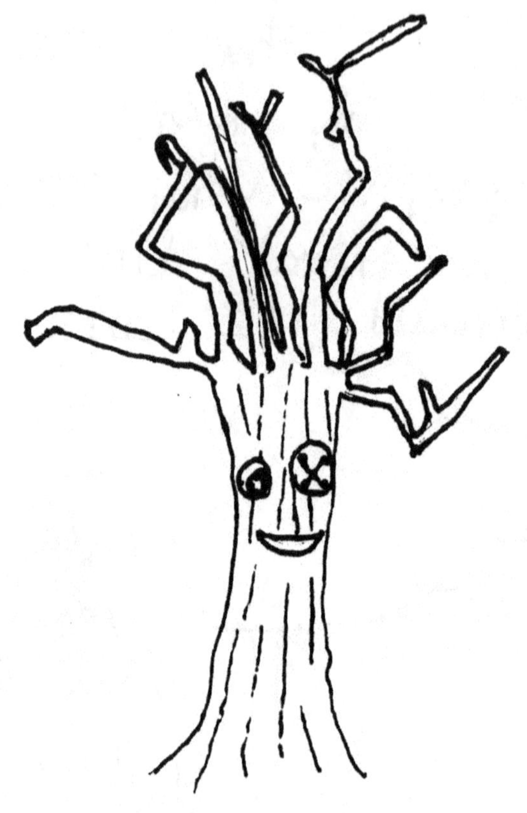

((tree of life))
Can you find it?

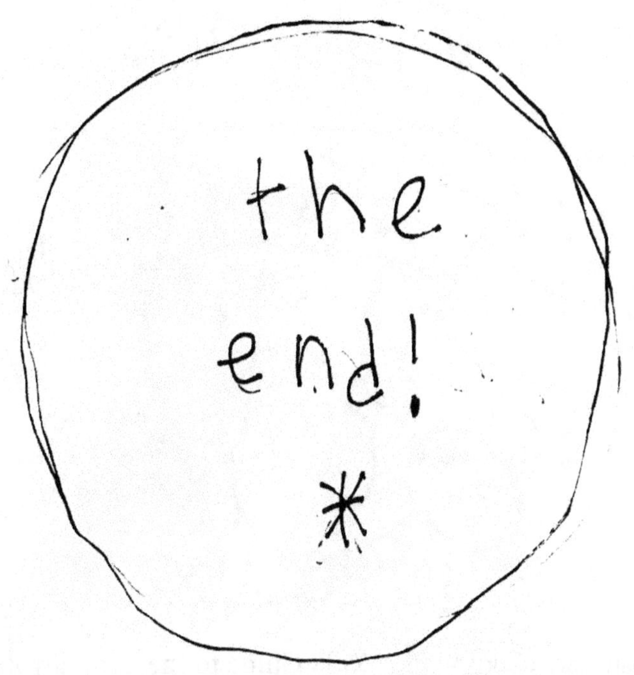
the
end!
*

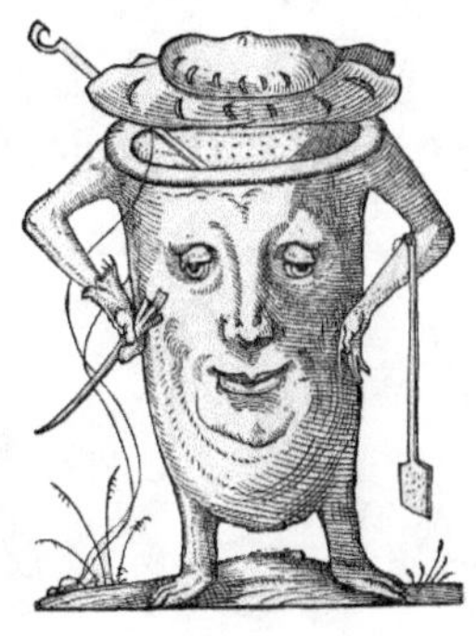

Alex Gaston visited the museum late in 2018 and was inspired to devote her Christmas vacation to the production of this guide for the upcoming generation of zymoglyphiles. She was seven years old at the time.

Spirits Under Glass

Photographs of the Zymoglyphic Museum
taken with the Zymo 127 pinhole camera

by Judith Hoffman

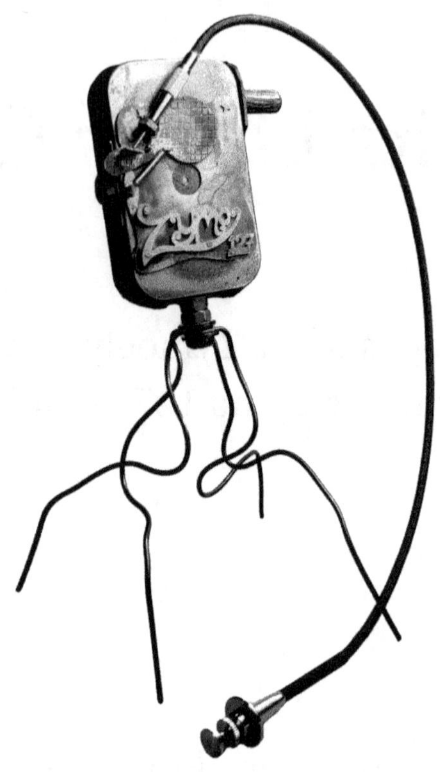

The Zymo 127 pinhole camera (brass, brass nut, steel spring, Altoids tin)
It takes 127 format film, which is cut down from 120
Tripod: brass bolt and nut, copper wire.

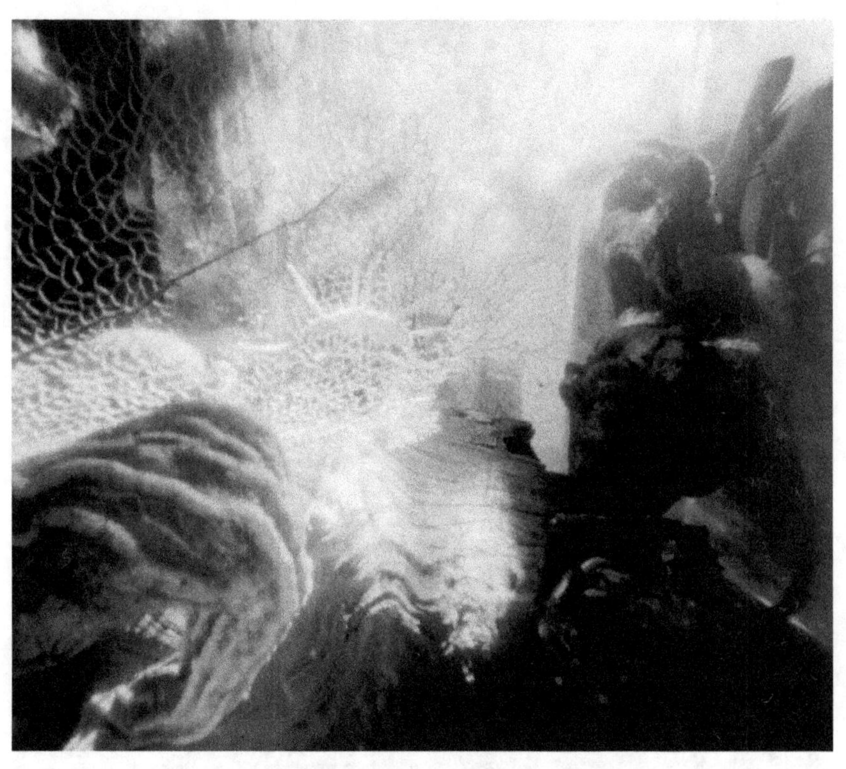

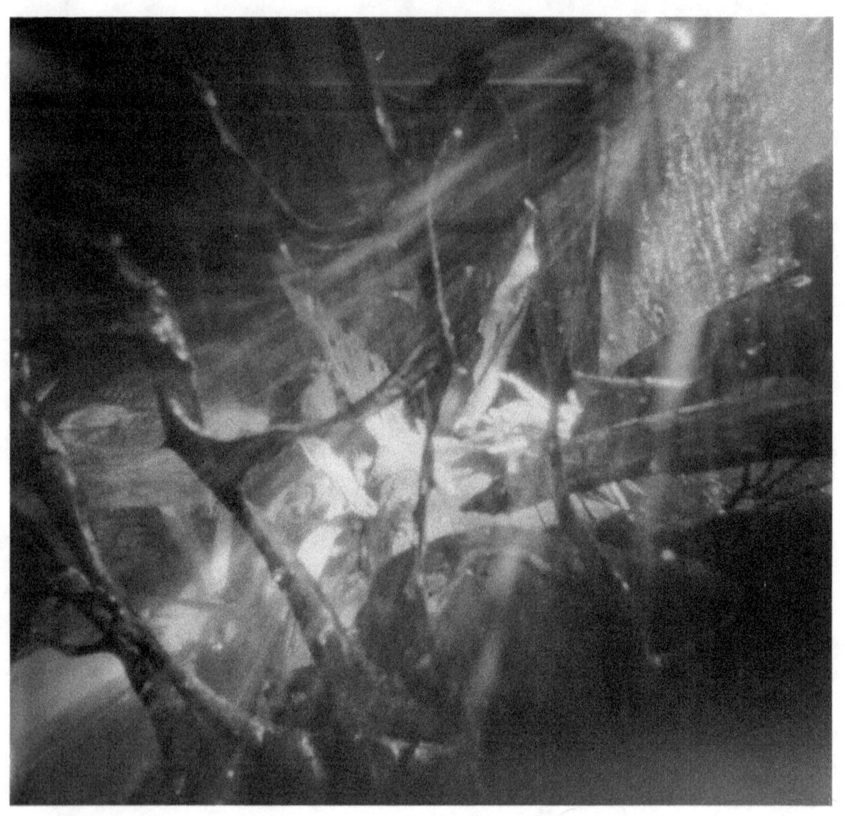

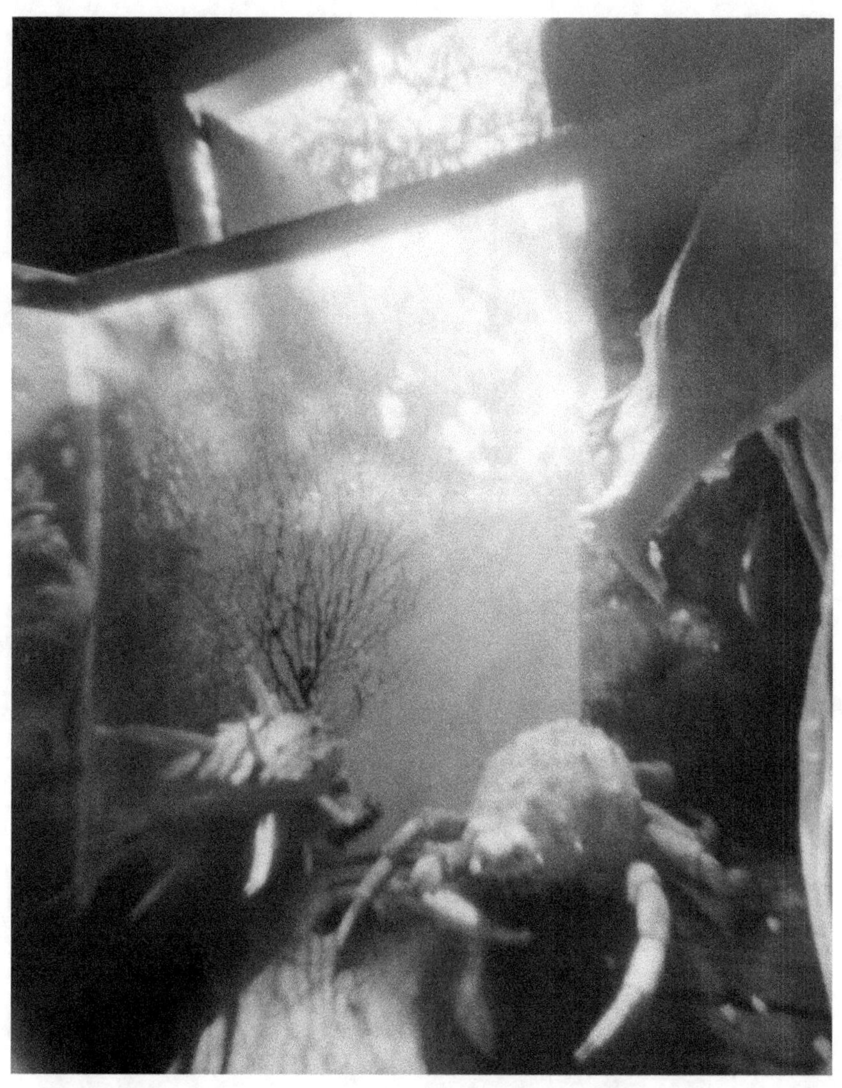

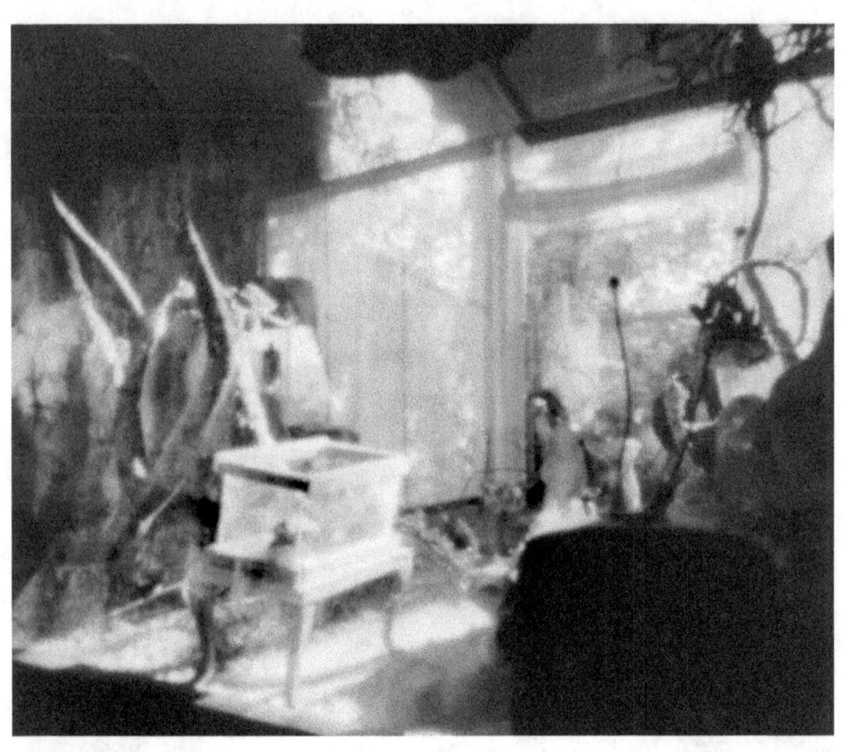

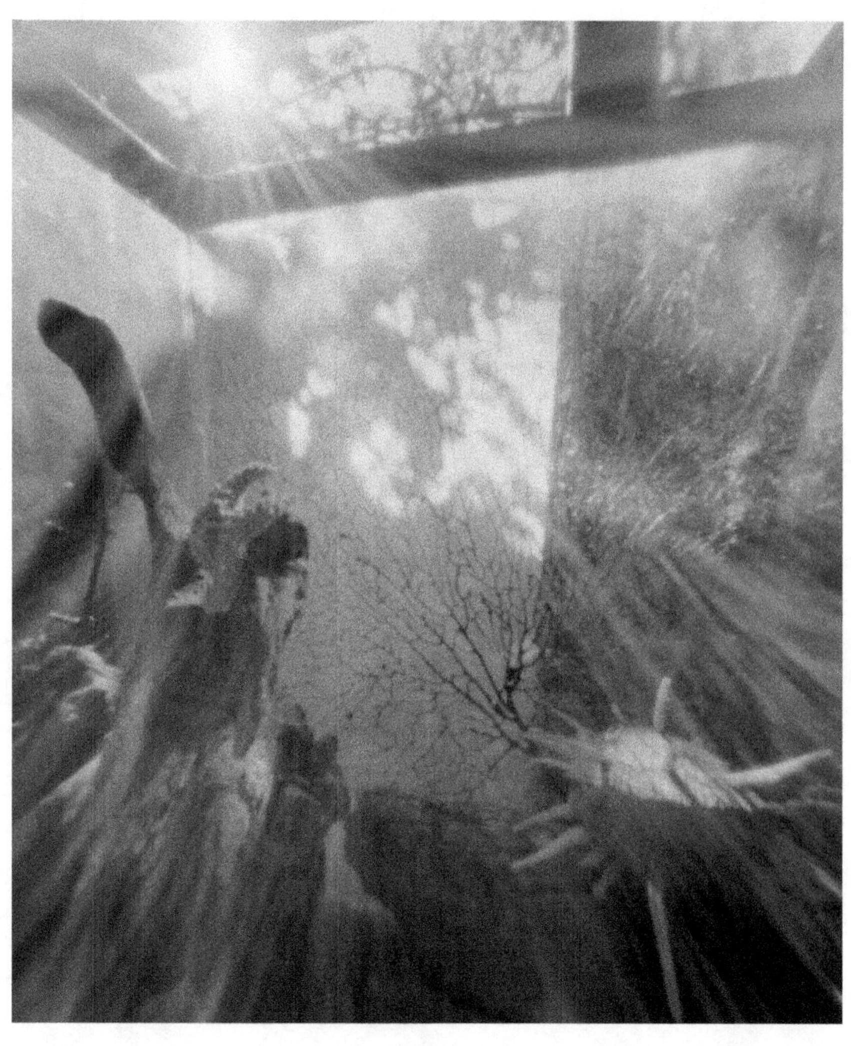

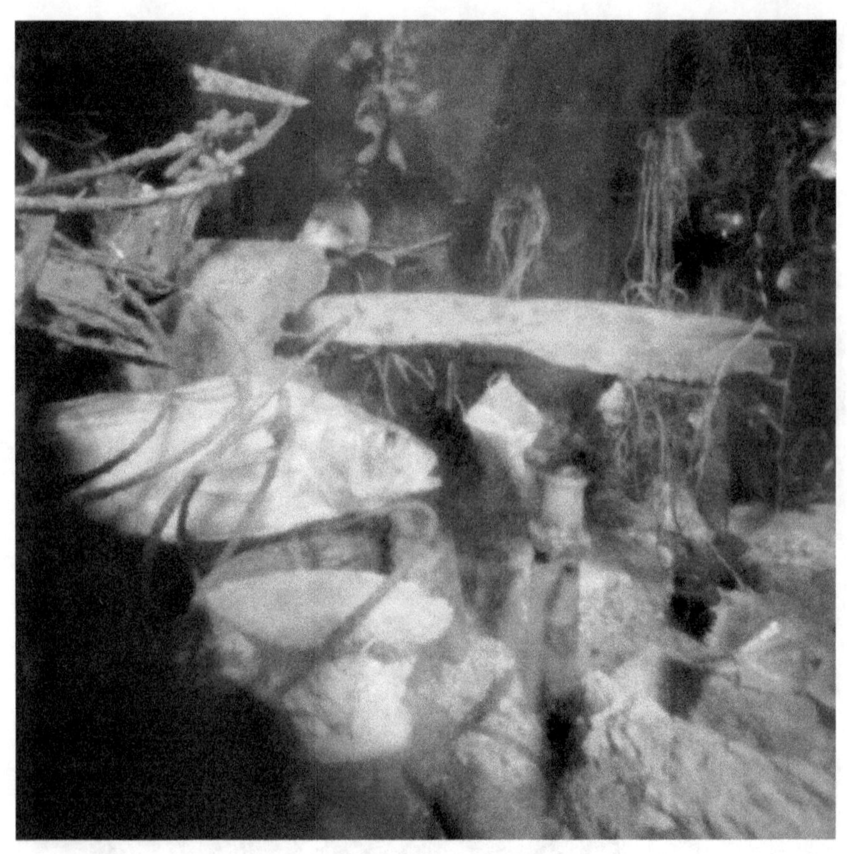

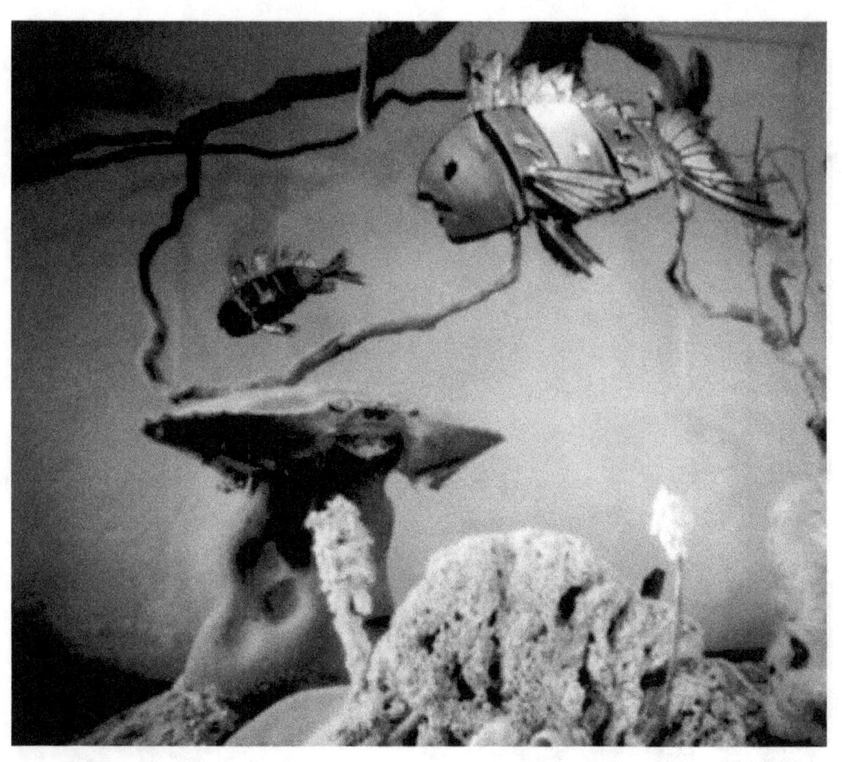

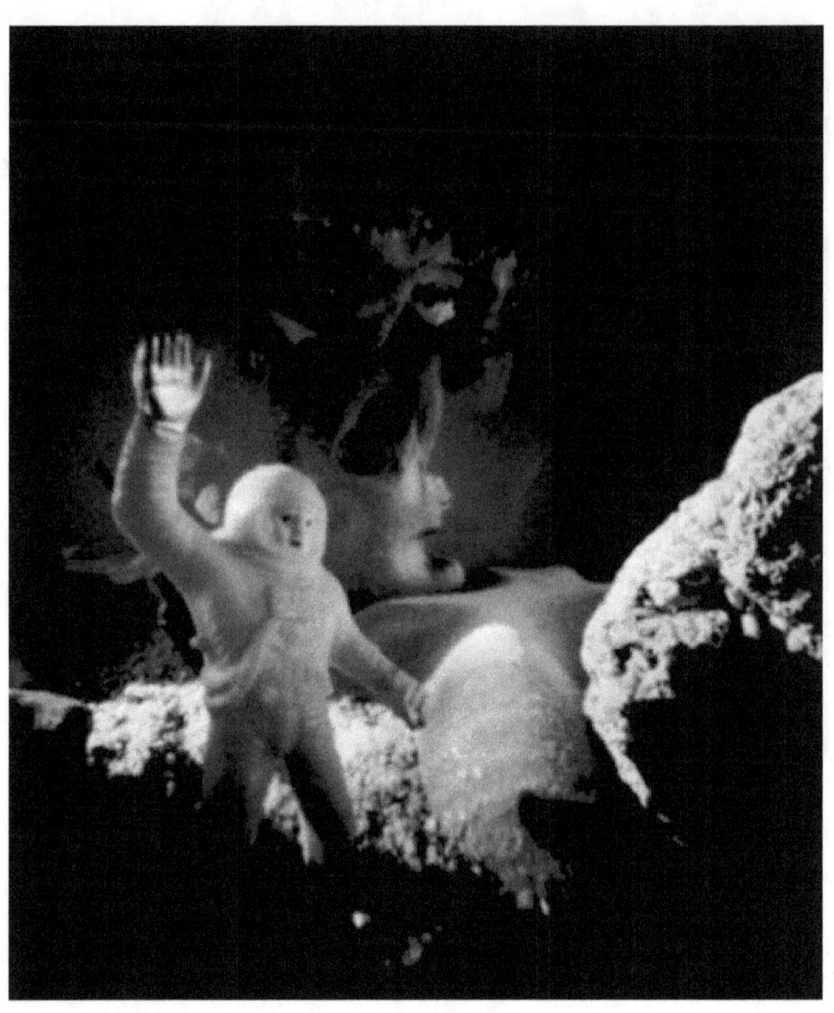

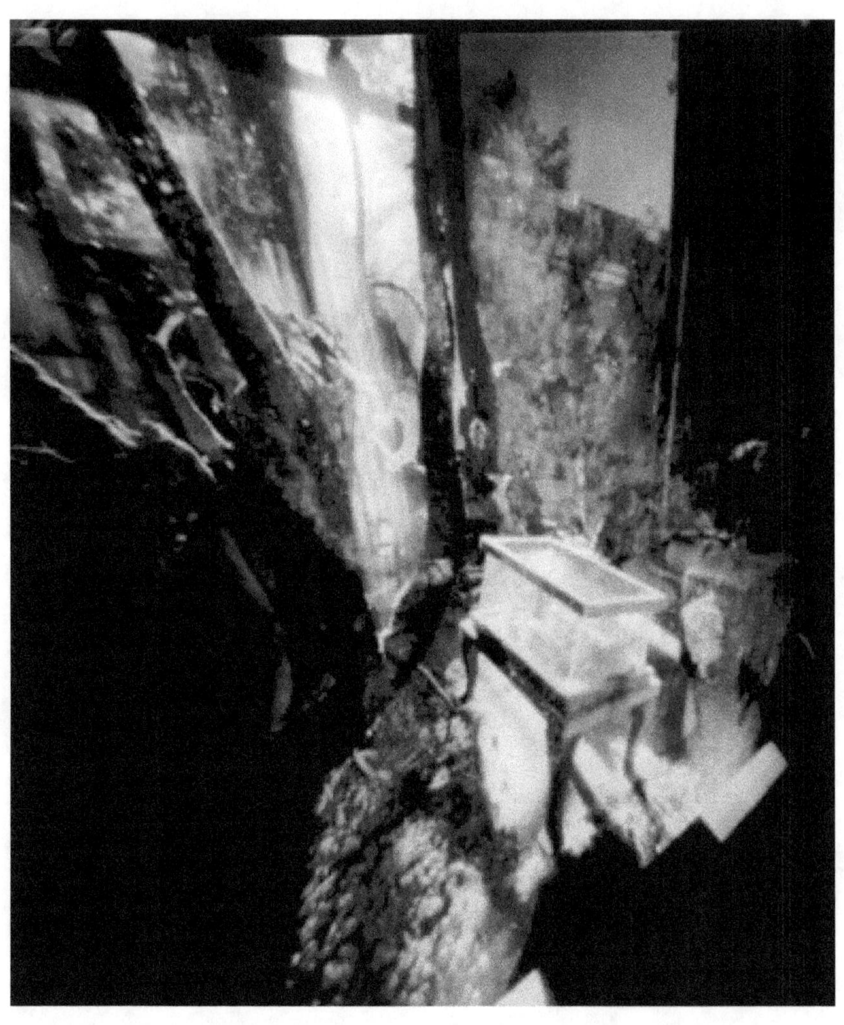

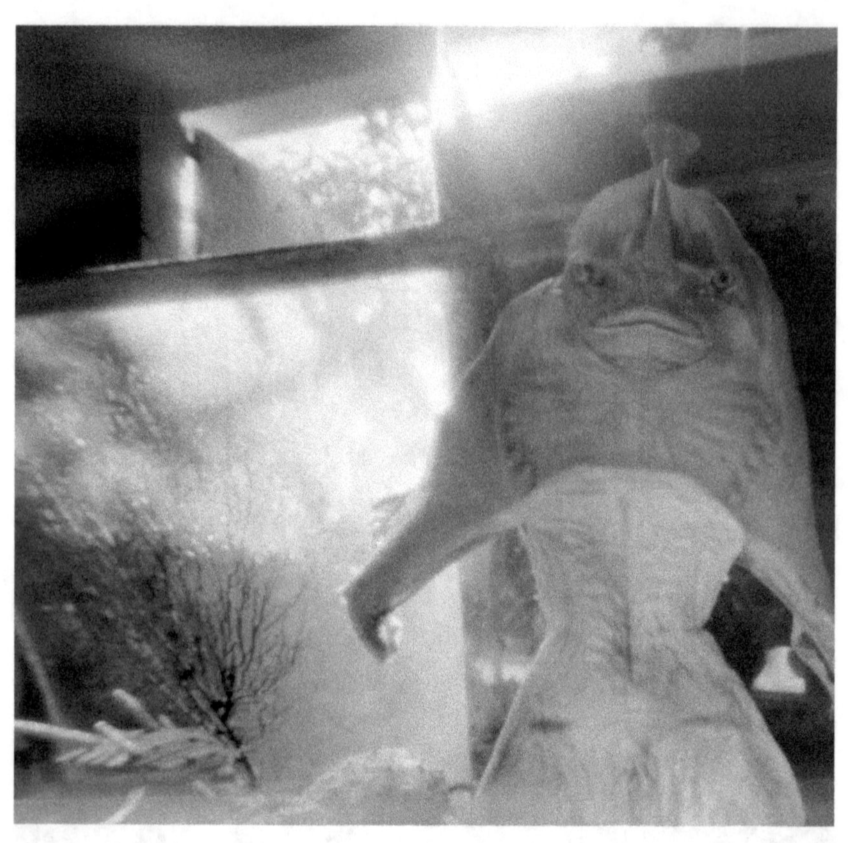

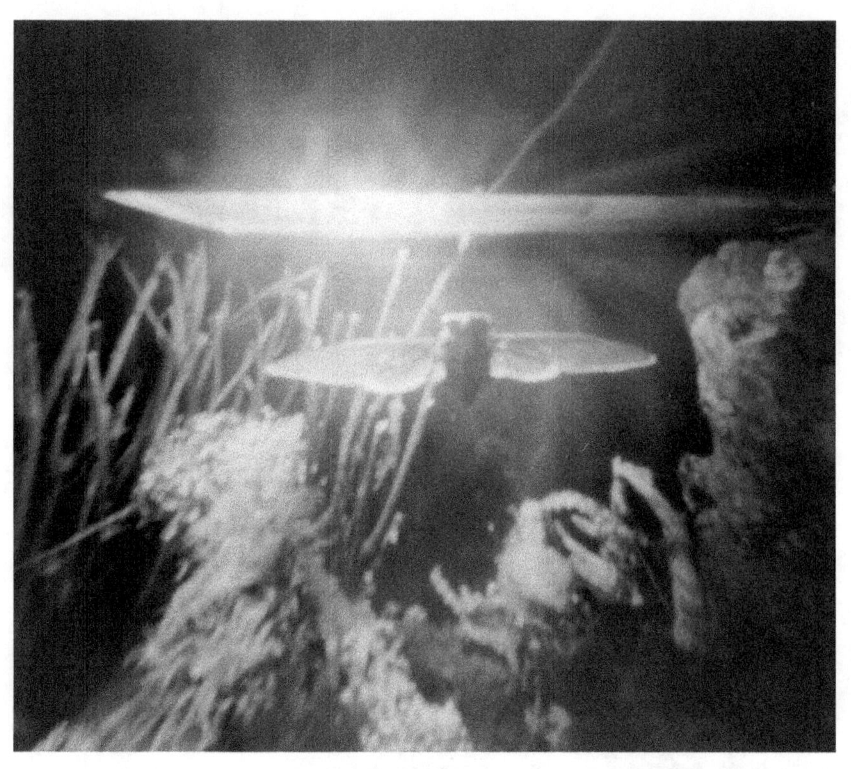

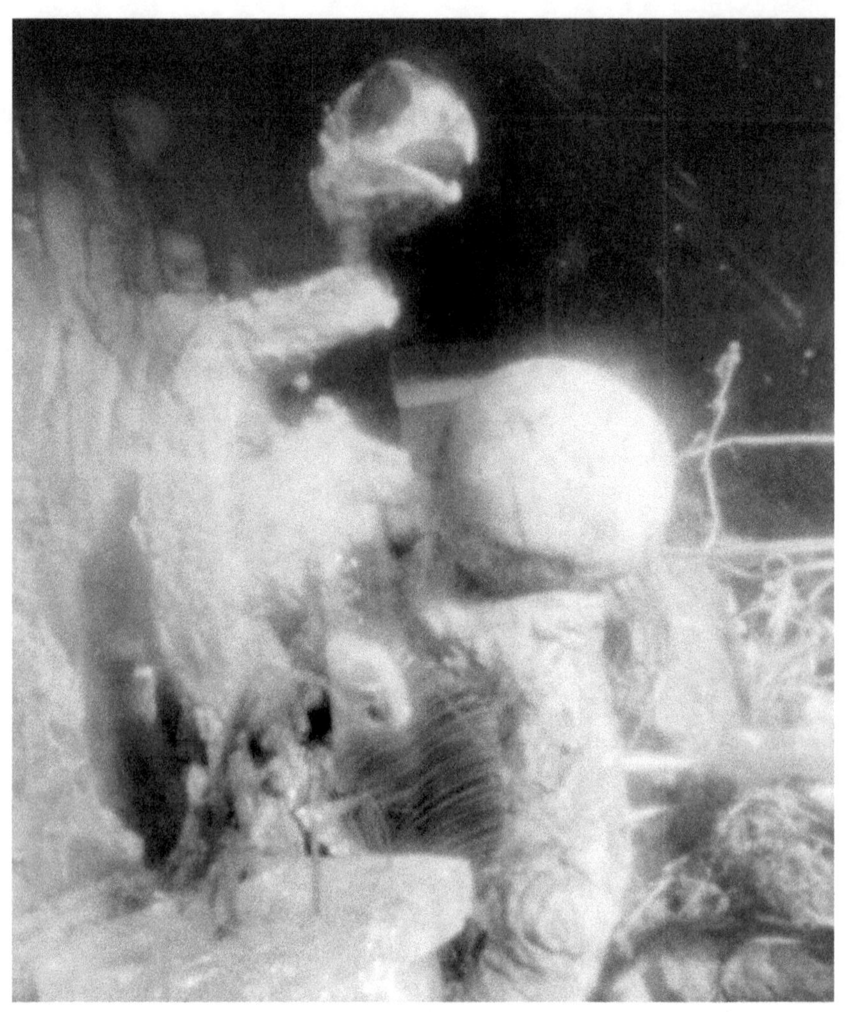

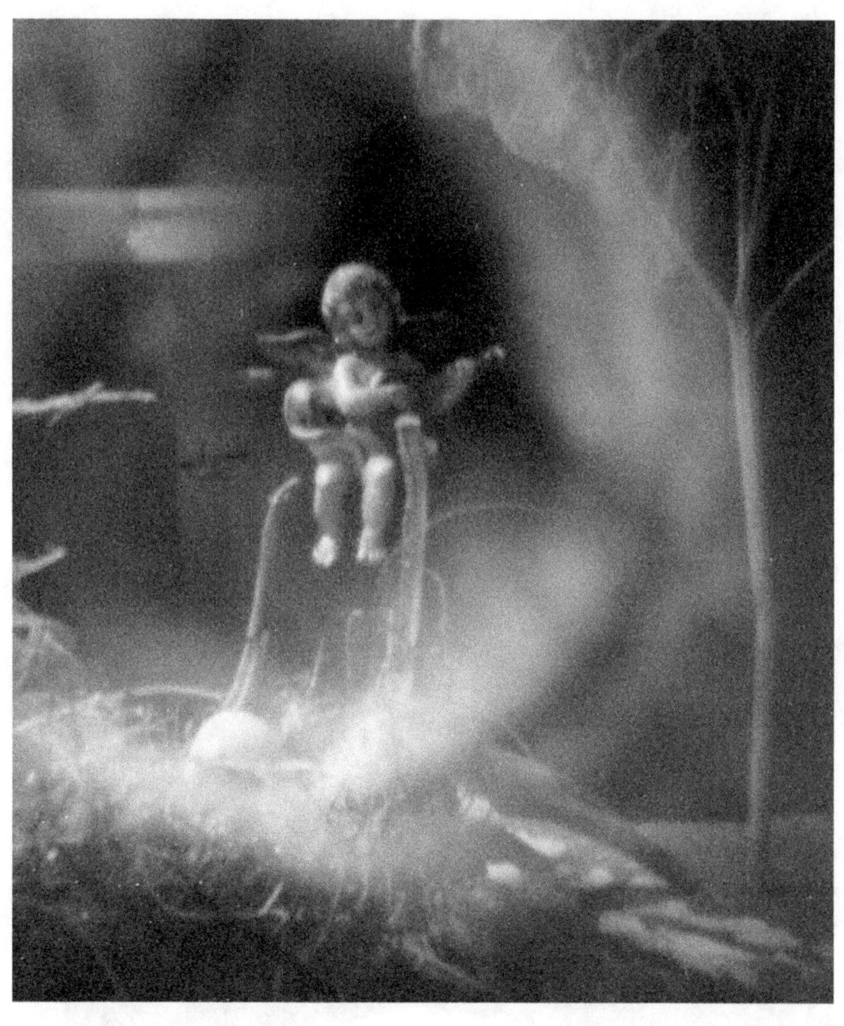

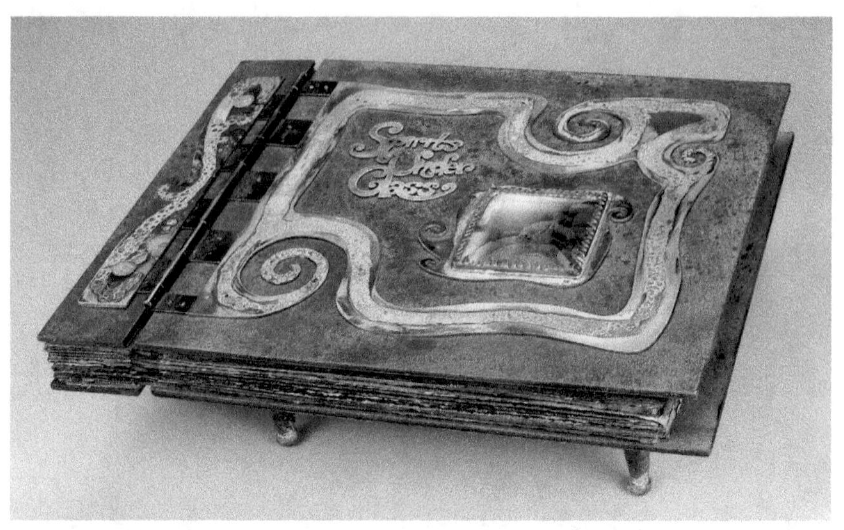

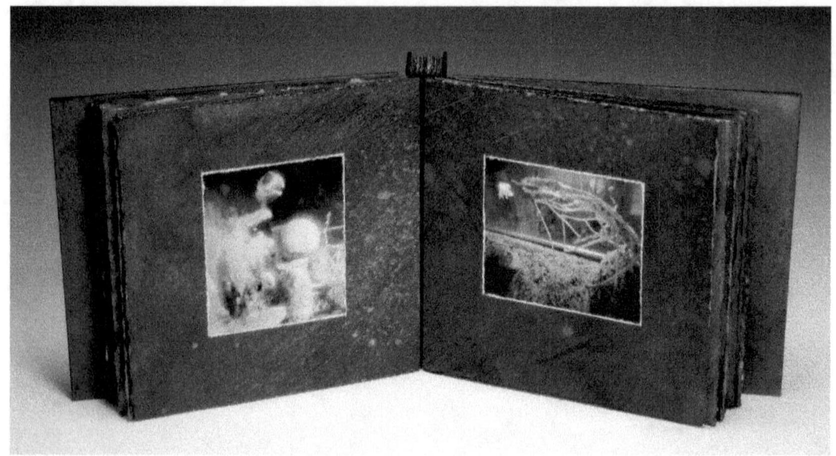

[*Spirits Under Glass* is a one-of-a-kind artist's book featuring photographs of the museum's dioramas and artifacts made with a purpose-made pinhole camera. These pages were selected from an unpublished trade edition of the project. -- Ed. note]

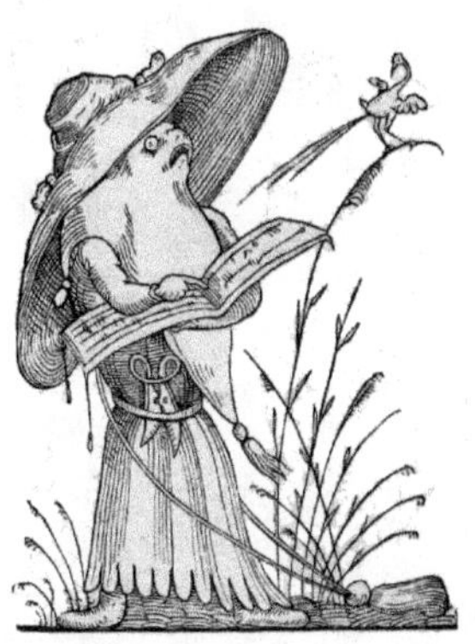

Judith Hoffman is a Portland-based book artist and artist-in-residence at the Zymoglyphic Museum. Her books are based on dreams, memories, and thoughts of death. To create the books, she combines collage, drawing, photography, and sometimes metalwork.

Judith's work can be seen at judithhoffman.net

Indestructible Object

&

the Zymoglyphic Moment

A story and a poem by
Jason Squamata

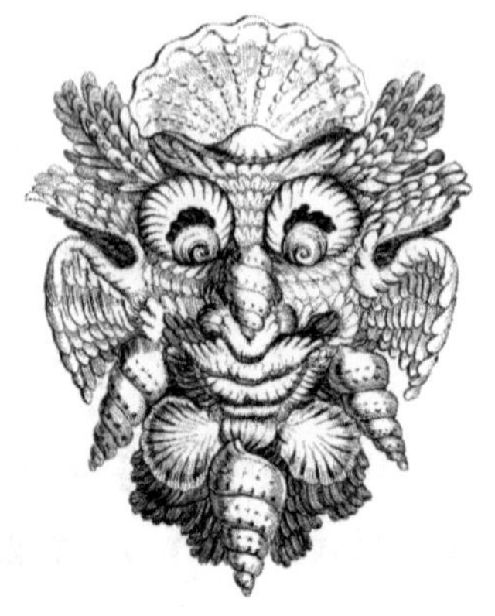

Indestructible Object

Sometimes I have people up to my cluttered apartment, where I am trying to figure all this out. Sometimes a friend. Sometimes a stranger. And they tend to ask me, sooner than later.

"What does Zymoglyphic mean?"

And it always shocks me. And I always flinch.

And I throw up my hands in a grandiose gesture that to me says "Behold! Take it all in!" And maybe I revolve a little. Slowly.

Indicating the scrapbooks and piles of documents that crowd every table, every counter, and most of the floor. Indicating the diagrams and collages of evidence that plaster the walls, as if it all maps a galaxy of madness. As if all this is the answer to that question.

But they would know it as such only if they have lived as I have lived and experience has trained them to make absurd associations, consuming these trajectories of circumstance through a crystalline analytical eye.

They would notice how all the chimera-riddled nautical maps and fetishistic photographs and odd assortments of rotting objects implode into the locus of HER.

A picture of her. My Violet. The woman I have known so deeply and who I now seek beyond the fields you know, unless you know what I know. In the crucible of her, I have known the Zymoglyphic like a fanatic knows his heaven.

A beauty so complete it boils me down to the act of seeing it.

No self left to question the vision or pretend to understand it.

She showed me this alien strain of beauty that blooms from the convulsive conjunction of antithetical frequencies. From the first, she embodied Otherness itself, a twilight place I'd only seen inside my own mind, where the will dissolves into dreaming.

Even when she seemed to be human.

Even when she seemed dull enough to love me.

She evoked the languor and dissipation of haunted jungles in the way she half-danced through a room like a prima somnambulist, in the way her gestures would mesmerize me utterly with no agenda whatsoever. Hypnosis for its own sake. Our trances were contiguous.

She was the Zymoglyphic vibration's very incarnation, moreso than I ever knew until it was just a little too late.

But I knew the vibration before her. I'd felt it before in diluted mutant forms.

When childhood games would take me someplace Other, through a door at the back of a daydream. Afternoons, evenings, whole summers lost in a spell of pretending. Lost in a book, in a story, in a game, my mind led someplace away from the body. A place as real as the body, but free of all physics. The constrictions of space. The texture of time.

When I would wander too deeply into those woods, those oceans, those worm-holy wardrobes…I left bits of myself on the other side of summer. When all joy and wild knowledge resides in trances and tricks of the feverish mind, consciousness cracks into craven catastrophe. I was always so homesick for wonderland that my ordinary waking world became a cage.

One step beyond into sensations you have no words for and a thought so big it bends your brain out of shape as you think it. Then you crave the cage. I...craved the cage. I kept it desperately real, for a time.

That's who and what and where I was when I saw her…really SAW her. I could already taste the medicines of the grim green rooms they would put me in. I'd be lying if I said I didn't hope she would destroy me.

And so she did.

But she left it unfinished. What's left of me yearns for a final swim in the abyss of her. My bouquet of beautiful bruises. My certain doom.

My Violet.

So I wandered too far afield that one time.

I had my little breakdown.

I decided to try taking the real world seriously. I developed methods of sublimating my Zymoglyphic urges. Having flinched from the abyss, I needed to convince myself (in a daily practice that became far too easy) that the rituals don't work and the games don't lead into secret worlds and what I saw on those powders and pills was a trick of light and chemistry.

I could still pick up on the vibration, in configurations that the layman might call "psychedelic" or "surreal". But I did not collect haunted objects to make altars or temples or museums like a curator does. I was a mere collector. A finicky consumer. My shadow cabinets were swollen not with accidental fragments of eternity but with mail order prefab pastiches of the miraculous.

My library indicates some kind of hardboiled mystic.

The images given pride of place suggest some kind of disturbed romantic.

Polymorphously erotic.

The social calendar indicates a slave.

In my post-gnosis trauma, I had assumed a compulsive pantomime of normality. I struggled to attune myself to the fundamental rhythm of the thundering world, the inhale exhale of the beast that eats all the days and nights of our lives and shits money as it feeds. Selling life-time cheaply all day. The nights reserved for wallowing in hungry mirrors that refused to reflect me.

For a little while, I thought I might be an artist or something. I could taste the nightside of Eden that way. Write books or something. Draw cartoons. A beloved entertainer. I've learned that this is a common mistake (or salvation) for the heretical heart that hungers after primal tactile knowledge of the mystery.

I had evaded my dreamy doom so expertly, SO artistically, with binges of narrative and little bags of money, grifting skills accrued like afterthoughts as I recoiled at every turn from the shadow of my becoming. Song and dance routines and radio games. Always unraveling at the brink of some success, knowing inwardly I was made for stages yet unbuilt, undreamt of even, stages known only to a shifty future self who has led me into being him with riddles.

In that inbetween time, I was living with a woman who I hoped would keep me sensible. Or MAKE me sensible, then keep me that way.

But then, in the midst of her, there was Violet. Violet Morton, she said.

Violet who I met in a gallery, sobbing and yet obviously oddly excited by a hovering holographic bolus of silver snakes, flexing endlessly. An orgiastic orgone orb for alchemists on the make. She was a certain type, to be sure. One of those nouveau wiccan hypnogoth alien beatnik mad scientist ballerina faerie queen women that you never see anywhere. The poise and dimensions of a catwalk robot mannequin, softening and uncoiling to touch things and make her day a ballet. Something spastic when I least expect it, like all that grace has been a parody of itself and I didn't get the joke.

A few years on, without her disturbance, I might have built a house of brick to keep the gold in me hidden and dead. But my safe house was made of paper, sudden flame in her dark, sleepy gaze. We spoke a cold poem that said everything. I didn't wonder if I should open the door she was. I only wondered, halfway through, how long I could keep up with her, how completely this would kill me.

The games began that very day. At the Looking Glass hotel, on Traducity Street. We discovered lingering virginities and took them from each other, with gratitude and just enough greed so we'd both know we were giving and taking the one thing that we need.

Despite my proclivities, despite the many kinks in the leash with which she tugged me, I'd been around the block one time too many, maybe, and my jadedness would sometimes pollute her basically ecstatic nature. Or I dreamed it did, and that would be bad enough to weird things.

We played all the sex games, or as many as acrobatic facts and physics would allow. We assumed sketchy identities and met again and again as strangers. Improvised psychodramas, recreational brainwashing scenarios, planting mutual memories through orchestrated gestalts of foreshadowing and flashback. Every rendezvous violently plugged into mythologies that were fraught with the erotics of anxiety.

We played all the drug games, chasing free epiphanies. The powders and crystals that engage an electric immersion in the moment. Hi-res texture mapped silver hysteria and the gradual atrophy of empathy. The tabs and pills and fungi that brought us both to the same sweet sanctuary of undulating psychedelic te-lepathy, the soul made visible and tactile in our fusion. The living languages that narrate all this, steaming and hissing through us in our melting, in our boiling, in our soft oneiric interface.

Those grains of hypersubstance, the decadimensional meta-language translator, sequins falling slowly from the beating sky-sized dragon wings of the great chaos. The sizzle and smoke that turned us inside out into ballrooms we will see again when we die, vaulted infinitudes running riot with angelic alphabets that wake up in us when we spell with them. When they saturate our sen-tences. A foaming gibberish that explains us to those who know that there is no knowing.

We wore the robes and chalked the circles and uttered the barbarous incantations. We opened doors in each other's heads, doors into the Zymoglyphic, though we did not yet know the word. We haunted the territory astrally, in lieu of its longitude and latitude. We summoned things and banished things. We divined things and projected things. We evoked and invoked the time-tested godforms that manifested most vividly in the unfold-ing of our lives.

We could slip into trances at the turn of a screw. We could channel savage presences on the altar, in the bed, on any available surface that could hold the weight of our brutally intimate religion. But even the ballrooms of Mars can decay into a maze of mutable memories and moonlit mossy cul-de-sacs. I knew a call to misadventure would come that I would not be man or superman enough to answer. A call that would sound to her like her destiny. The best one yet.

That call came at yet another gallery.

Something about the vision of Violet in a state of gazing seemed to draw people into her spooky circumference. Something about the way she seemed to shiver and burn for any rare thing that was as lovely and as strange as her reflection.

She was handed an engraved invitation by a thoroughly bandaged woman in dark glasses and a bespoke suit. A bowler hat. A totemic umbrella. A London banker burn victim refugee from some economic holocaust in progress. I never read the papers before cutting them up into poetry. So I just wouldn't know. The invitation was addressed to Violetta Muerte and One Other of her choosing. An opening soiree at the Zymoglyphic Museum. The bandaged woman was gone before we could ask her what Zymoglyphic means. The word seemed somehow ominous in print, and electric on our tongues as we uttered it. Like licking live batteries.

I could tell from Violet's quizzical gaze into space that she had already decided that she would answer to "Violetta Muerte" if it meant getting into a mad party, and that "Zymoglyphic" might be the magick word my slumming faerie goddess had been looking for.

Oh, that most enchanted of ceremonies, the spangling of the self for a night of mad celebration.

I can't account for the heartbreak of every young lover, but in my experience, on the night when you know it's over, you know before it happens. Its gravity haunts you backwards from the bitter moment to come. It was like that, Violet and I getting tarted up for the opening.

Or maybe it was the gloom of pure mortality. In prettier times, I'd get into it, the conjuring of glamour, but the haggard years of chasing butterflies through wheat threshers were just starting to take their toll on me. Violet could seem to be ancient in a certain mood, but she was young enough for me to wonder in weaker moments if I was in her way or just a phase, despite our seeming symbiosis.

And of course, on that night, for that party, she had never looked so beautiful, to an inner eye in me that was already moist from missing her, despite her feckless grin and her insistence that this was just another shocking episode in our bizarre love story, and not the finale. She looked like a black cherry carcrash. I was disguised as a housefire. We took a taxicab to the happening.

I'm not sure what I expected. My sense of local neighborhoods and my physical environment in general was always nebulous at best. I assumed we'd be pulling up to some edgy-ish downtown street gallery or an industrial space, a converted slaughterhouse or something. I knew art openings from books, mostly. Never got out much, except with her. But our cab pulled up to a house. A charming suburban house, so unassuming, the garage door open, all the lights on. An elegant fiftysomething gentleman at the threshold, welcoming a succession of very special guests. He was dressed in tweed like the professor of something, with a panting hothouse lily pinned to his lapel, the silver beard and questioning eyes of some Socrates, spectacles tinted with a substance that sees through you. When he inspected the invitation and realized he was in the presence of THE Violetta Muerte, he came to life, like he'd heard so much about her and he loved her work.

I wondered what her work might be like as I played second fiddle to the hilt. We had discussed the possibility that a genuine Violetta Muerte would arrive without her invite and spoil every-thing, but Violet was convinced that the poetic distortion of her name was no coincidence, and that she was somehow meant to be here. Then she corrected herself. WE are meant to be here. But I was barely an observer, from the beginning. She was just being nice. So I felt like half a sidekick, half a sacrifice. Nothing to see here, Zymoglyphic party people. Just a trembling shadow cast by a strangely famous woman as she slips into the shimmer of a world I'll never know.

The garage first, the evolving shrines, the altars in progress, art books with accounts of previous seekers, art cults of yesterday that have since been commodified and absorbed by the spectacle, except in works whose fundamental obsessive Otherness cannot be digested. Those works form an anti-matter canon. Presumably these are jigsaw fragments of the Zymoglyphic Enigma. Despite my alienation, I could empathize with Violet's excitement. This place and the people in it might be everything I told her I was looking for. Artifacts from other Earths. Technologies smuggled from an interstitial space between the abrasive waking world and the bottomless dream. Allegorical collages and deconstructed relics and carefully edited popular editions of fundamental Zymoglyphic scriptures.

A trashy looking pulp paperback for sale called HOTEL ZYMOGLYPHIC.

The cover gave me vertigo for reasons that are clearer to me now.

I was afraid to touch it. But Violet wasn't afraid of anything… but my fear. She was flipping through it, skipping to the end. The Curator interrupted her peek at our denouement, ushering us to a steep, crooked stairwell. Were we the last to arrive? I could taste the red threads of Violet's magickal thinking, without a word. Maybe we're the guests of honor. Maybe the party couldn't start without us. Maybe this is in fact some kind of cult. How interesting. We could hear the wingtip and stiletto clatter and the sophisticated laughter of fancy people who were up the stairs, ahead of us. As we started climbing, the stairwell seemed to flex like some macrocosmic orifice, happy at last to be filled with us.

The Curator, right behind me, started laughing.

So already there was this funhouse feeling.

The lighting was vaguely radioactive.

I was having tactile flashbacks to ancient claustrophobias.

The air smelled funny, each breath alive with tantalizing microbes.

I couldn't tell if it was some exotically authentic incense, smoke from some drug I'd never heard of, or a mélange of expensive customized perfumes, but it was going to my head. I reached ahead of me to touch Violet's hip and steady myself. In the paranoid discomfort of the moment, her hand on mine felt like a rebuke. Those domino moments that lead to despair were falling already.

The glass cases that lined the stairwell were squirming with segmented mermaid parts. Jellyfish with pretty female faces. Sea monkey jungles running riot with infestations of tadpole people. Plaques too busy to read in the half-light. Climbing towards the museum itself, which seemed small at first, small and crowded with the luminaries of this inscrutable Zymoglyphic clique.

It was not so much a party as a dream about parties. When a strange space, cluttered with miracles, is full of people you don't know, and the one you're there with, you know her less and less, and everyone speaks in a slang you've never heard about things that confuse you. The names you recognize are traps that make you want to show them how smart you are, but this isn't a place for collectors, only practitioners. And the experts have no mercy.

People wearing nightmare masks turn out to be disfigured. Others unzip their faces and turn out to be all mask. There are dainty little cabinets spilling over with precious objects. Each aggregation seems to be heavy with a meaning that eludes you. But Violet gets it. You can see her commune with every piece of deliberate or accidental art she sees. She divines the object's secret life and feels it deeply. And you can see the sophisticated wolfish eyes of the men and women here, seeing her for what she is and peeling her secretly and you can't communicate the building menace without making demands, without holding her back.

A cluster of screens host a virtual ecology, looping the first algebra to arise from the primordial ooze, generating a chaos of fractalizing lifeforms, an orgiastic fecundity churning and swooning in the depths of an imaginary ocean. The Zymoglyphic

Enigma in miniature. A teratoma of misshapen microcosms. And she is the broken belle of the ball and the only art lovers in this chamber of latent horrors who don't want a piece of her are the monsters who want the whole thing.

In a curiously crooked corner, I lose track of her somehow, dizzy from the metalevels at work in the nesting dioramas. I approach the Curator, hoping for an indication of her whereabouts, but he has no time for the likes of me. None of them do. Their gossip suggests the existence of a secret world or several, filled to their fringes with unfortunate miracles. I can only talk about my esoteric shopping habits. And the fragrant vapors are still much too thick.

Are these rotting boxes of junk alive somehow?

Clip art scribbles, curdling into the atavistic.

Stop motion seizures in the stairwell again, looking for undoctored air to breathe, gasping for a taste of outside.

And you want to go home but she was invited here on purpose and she gets it all and she wants more.

You want to go home and she would rather not and everything you say here comes out sideways and is the intelligent, malevolent ambience warping all your signals on purpose?

You want to go home and she won't go home and she hates that you're making her choose and you are leaving anyway.

Dismembered mermaids laughing as you stumble down the flexing staircase, which seems to spit you into the street. You stagger home and settle down and you becomes me again and I am waiting for too many minutes, waiting for her to finish becoming herself so she can come home to me and tell me everything.

But she didn't. She did come home before dawn, but quietly, like she didn't want to talk about what happened there, like she preferred not to wake me, like she couldn't even look at me. All she told me was that she would be going back. There was nothing I could do about that. I was getting used to a new way of being alone in the uneasy dark before her dawn.

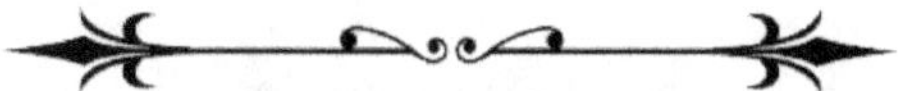

There's a surrealist object Man Ray made called "indestructible object". It's a totemic fetish dedicated to Lee Miller, his famously brilliant and beautiful muse and collaboratrix. They had enjoyed a season of mutual fanatical adoration, but Lee was a free spirit, a younger woman who was finding herself artistically in the mad Paris of the 30s and she was naturally compelled to spread her butterfly wings. She would be out having strange adventures with other surrealists and aristocrats and criminal types, while Man Ray punished the floorboards of their flat with his ceaseless pacing. He fastened a sphinxish photograph of her eye to the tip of a metronome. He would set it after one of their more and more frequent quarrels, the second she stepped out for the evening with the clatter of heels and a sudden slam. The object would harshly count the lonely moments until she came home to him. As the hours eventually became days, he added a component to the piece. A hammer in repose. Like it's a kit. Like it's a gnomic inversion of his early assemblage, the Enigma of Isidore Ducasse. This arrangement of objects equals chronophobic immersion in time and the desperate suffocation of the spirit, consumed by its own regrets and insecurities. When she left for good he renamed it: "Object To Be Destroyed".

I wouldn't call Man Ray's attitude aspirational, but it is relatable. I dig it all too deeply. So I get a metronome and I make my own object, with a Violet eye, scissored from a big picture of the two of us, happy. Just like I made my own dream machine, and my own ghost radio. Finding new ways to get lost in her, even when she's barely here.

She is more and more deeply involved in her Zymoglyphic demimonde. After that first party, she asked me along once or twice as a courtesy, but we both knew my chance at the garden had been thwarted by my fear, by my fundamentally self-involved and cowardly nature. A simultaneous desire to possess her and self-loathing over having no real attractions to seduce her with. Just a lot of talk. And an apartment where she left all of her things.

At first, she makes weak attempts to describe what goes on at these meetings of hers. The Zymoglyphic Society. I can tell that she's afraid my envy and estrangement will make me lash out at a fragile metaphysical system that maybe hasn't quite yet settled in her all too eager head. That small fear in her is the only power I have left, it seems. So I savor it and learn nothing.

She comes home with the strangest bruises sometimes. And lipstick traces in the strangest places. Tasting faintly of other people. I knew these expeditions of hers would take a turn for the erotic, if they hadn't already on that first night. This is the first gate of understanding. This futile fury, this delusion that when she adored me and I seemed to understand her I had some ownership of her affections. I had enjoyed her beauty like it was something I earned with my expertly performative empathy. It breaks me to know that every other night she is engaged in in-novative tantric configurations with people much cooler than me, doing things we read about together but had never attempted.

A painful scenario, to be sure, with me still paying all the rent and whatnot, but it only stabs at my core when she comes in just before dawn with an especially numinous nimbus of dream bubbles, fairy lights, and auric echoes of last night's artificial paradise. Tittering and singing in tongues at first and then remembering the objects of her relinquished waking life, remem-bering me and our distances and her tears catch flecks of glitter in their trickling. I hate the mornings when it seems like she's been someplace perfect that it hurts her to return from. I often wonder why she bothers, but to ask directly might deny me the privilege of her sobbing proximity, my only joy, when she is too tired to hide from me and I can listen to her breathe in the ach-ing early half-light.

I can abide her sexual transgressions and her delirium. We were obsessively monogamous for so long, we have no language with which to negotiate these transmutations, and even if we did, her speech patterns are increasingly fragmented into whispery sheets of witchy poetry. All I can do is work in the world and pay the rent and be here to catch her and comfort her when she flies too close to some atomic memory and comes home broken.

But today she comes in softly, climbs into bed beside me, making noises I can't identify until I realize she is sweating birds.

Little sparrows.

Squeezing themselves into being through pores in her dewslick skin and fluttering madly around the bedroom.

I throw open the window and hope they make it out there and I gaze with fresh purpose on her primordially fertile skin, her careless limbs somehow elegant, even in jumbled repose. I can indulge her every damage and my own crippling issues if this is just a game of sex and drugs and patience, but if she's gone all wrong in ways that are impossible, if the physics that hold her time and space together start breaking down, I know that my quiet courage is just another shade of terror, and if I love her at all I will need to protect her from the creepy junkyard voodoo of the Zymoglyphic nightlife.

So today I'm bringing food into the bedroom and locking her in it while I walk around the block and think about who to call about something like this. General practitioner or ornithologist? Cult deprogrammer or freakshow impresario? I decide the first step is to nurse her through the kicking of whatever bizarre appetites she has acquired amongst her new friends. If we can just recalibrate our frequency and speak the same language and stop sweating birds, we can talk about what a coward I've been and how I'm here to build a bridge for her back to reality. I'm imagining a renaissance of our boyfriend-girlfriend frequency. Staying away from the spooky stuff. Writing more things for money. This could be just what we needed, this Zymoglyphic detour, and we learned a lot, but maybe it's time to get back on that royal road to things that people want. Her disintegration has cured me of my hunger for the marvelous. I'm ready to say that. It should wait until after her withdrawal, but maybe I'll say it now just as a prelude she can look back on when she hangs heavy with child and we laugh about how weird we were, before the birds.

She's gone somehow when I get back to the flat, of course.

Three flights up. It couldn't have been the window. No damage to the door. Another unfortunate miracle.

There is a sparrow, though.

It tweets expectantly, as if appointed to receive the words of love I prepared in lieu of vanishing Violet. I know where there's a hammer but I resist the urge to make sparrow jelly. Instead I set the metronome and I shrink beneath her paper gaze and I breathe her sheets and the ticking is my heartbeat. Beating for no reason til she comes back to me.

But she doesn't come back.

Not the next day. Not the next week. Not the week after that,

It seems like I'm the only one who notices. Our involvement was so intense that I let most of my friendships wither by the wayside, and no one that I currently call a friend has ever met her. And she had no family. And few friends of her own. Transient people, I'm realizing in this, the longest of her absences, how tenuously she was tethered to life. From before the beginning.

I've decided it's time to revisit the Zymoglyphic Museum. In broad daylight. I make some inquiries. Aside from the special evening events reserved for the Society and those that the Society invites, the museum is open to the public every other Sunday. And on this Sunday, it all looks so different in the daylight. All of the curiosities so enchanting and inviting, no hint of menace, no threat or promise of secret knowledge. A quirky creative space you can bring the kids to. And there are children here, attuned already to the dollhouse logic of it all, making faces at the mermaids. And the curator is here, out of his tweeds, in casual clothes, less like hemlocked Socrates and more like the eccentric uncle you always wanted. His eyes twinkle on contact with mine.

"Why hello. You've been here before, haven't you?"

"I have, yes. I have a friend who comes here quite a lot, actually. Violet. I think she's in your 'society'."

I search his face for hints of her dark fate and any residual tics of complicity. There's only warm enthusiasm. Authentic joy or a brilliant disguise.

"You mean Violetta Muerte! Of course! One of our darkest stars! You must be Jason Squamata."

The name strikes a chord that upsets me.

"Actually, no. That sounds a little like my name…"

"Or vice versa."

"Is this how you do it, then? Am I invited into your cult now? No engraved invitation for me? Are you giving me a special cult name to throw me off the scent?"

"Ha! Always so paranoid with those noirish undertones. We love your work. As for 'the scent', what exactly might you be sniffing around for?"

"For Violetta. For Violet. I'm looking for Violet. I haven't seen her in weeks. Has she been around?"

"Ms. Muerte booked passage on the S.S. Interloper two weeks ago. She seemed very flustered at the time, said someone tried to put her in a cage. It seemed to be a matter of the utmost urgency. So I accepted her fare and sent her to receive her rightful reverence in the Zymoglyphic Region. I'm sure she's relaxing there as we speak. Relieved of all care. Free as a bird."

"The Zymoglyphic Region? The imaginary place you made out of all these horrible objects? What are you talking about ? The S.S. Interloper?"

"Yes. A ghost ship that collects the initiate in dreams when they have paid their fare."

"Violet didn't have any money."

"Money is for slaves. You pay your way aboard with a story. A story of whatever path brought you to the Zymoglyphic."

"…and then what?"

"Then the spectral sailors take you away from all this."

"You're insane. You're ALL insane. Where the fuck is my girlfriend?"

I see a dangerous will rise almost to his surface, but the hosting face is resumed as those kids come clambering down the stairs. They eye my wound-up body language suspiciously. He

gives them souvenirs and plays the wise and harmless schtick to
the hilt. I consider forcing the issue then and there, in front of
his public. The sunlight splashing the open gate seems somehow
more desolate than the howling starry night that churned above
my last visit. I let them leave. It would be all too easy for him to
pass me off to passersby as a belligerent, unstable street person,
despite the fact that all the gibberish has been his.

"Your girlfriend, Mr. Squamata? That's not the way she described you in her story."

"My name…never mind. Let me read her story."

"It's packed with confidential information that would only
confuse you, I'm afraid. But worry not. Her affection for you
was real, and she'll no doubt be visiting you from time to time, if
you still have all her things. Our cherished objects tie us to the
phenomenal world with silken threads of association."
"She'll be visiting? Visiting…from the Zymo fucking Glyphic
region?"   "Yes. The territory is sponge-like, in a sense.
Riddled with holes. Holy with riddles. Problem is, if you don't
sail back or forth on the Interloper, a hole could lead anywhere.
Twenty years after the beloved is gone. Three weeks before you
met them. Maybe some sideways time where everything turned
out differently. So she could turn up anywhen. Transformed, I
suspect. When was the last time you saw her?"

"I told you. Weeks ago. Here's what I think. I think this
magic toyshop bullshit is a cover for some sick drug cult that
attracts a certain type. I might have been that certain type, but
you couldn't seal the deal with me. My instincts are too good. I
thought I was afraid, but I was just being smart. You got Violet
though, used her for god knows what, twisted her in so many
directions that her hallucinations are infectious. Did you use her
all up? Did you tell her the ghost ship is coming to get her when
you drugged her and chopped her up for some snuff film connois-
seur?"

"…as I said, Squamata. I love your work, partly for the over
the top gruesome slant of your imagination, so this theory is par
for the course, but frankly, I find your speculations offensive."

"I wonder if the police will find my speculations offensive."

"You should go home and come to your secret senses, Squa-mata. You've come down with a bad case of gritty realism. Be careful lest that in committing to common sense, you occlude yourself from the kingdom."

"Is the kingdom where you bury the bodies? If you hurt her…"

"That was your job. Come back when you're ready, Squa-mata."

"I'll come back with police."

"If that's the ending that pleases you. We're closed for the day."

His hand on my shoulder as he leads me out is a caring hand, like he's gently guiding a friend from the party when he's had too much to drink. He's closing the garage door in my face and I'm a quantum ghost in his driveway. I'm either in a heartbreaking true crime nightmare or an utterly implausible fairytale. Despite everything, I want to live in a world where I get to decide which is true.

The police don't want to hear it, as it turns out. The curator is a respected member of the community. Violetta Muerte or Violet Morton or Viola Manson, as it turns out, was such a compulsive wanderer that she's just a few photographs shy of being a fig-ment of my imagination. And in my struggles, I have this creep-ing suspicion that wherever she is, in some collage of heaven or some forensic hell, she likes it this way, becoming more and more imaginary every day.

The birds become more and more real, though. She's sweat-ing them again, in the dream I have every night, in the wrecked apartment that was once a bizarre bower of bliss for us, a funky bohemian playpen, now just a dissection chamber for my de-ranged investigation. And there's a din of restless feathers when-ever I wake up from her, and last night the dream was deep and wet and we were one organism again, her craziest skin riding my sin and receiving me again, in such a fever that the sparrows

emerged in their thousands and pecked us all to pieces and the
story she wrote to escape this brutal world, she knew it by heart
and she recited it in my ear and in the torment of blood and
beak and talon and in the rapture of interface with my object of
longing, I understood that I never knew her.

She thought I might know her, every now and then, and she
could not name what I could not give her but the lack of it was
killing her. My game of her was abstraction at first sight, and
as she slipped through me from ravishing madwoman who will
haunt me to good witch who will save me to reflection who will
eat me with her greedy dreams to harsh mistress who owns me in
absentia…I never really let her speak. In the most exacting retro-
spect, I find my descriptions of her flirtations and breakdowns
and confessions, but not the words. Wherever and whatever she
is now, I want my life to have been a frame for words that are
hers.

So I woke up with a knowing. Not a knowing that she is alive,
but a knowing that I won't hear her voice on this side of summer
again. I'm not yet a fanatic. I haven't been to all those parties. I
haven't smoked all that fungus. But I am nothing without knowing her in her truth. My memoir is nothing without a transcription of her testimony, stripped of my distortions and projections.
And there is in fact an engraved invitation under my pillow.
Made out to Jason Squamata. My Zymoglyphic name, I suppose. Whatever that means.

Even if that fire in the curator's eye is in fact madness and this
account only buys me a drugged slumber and a shovel to the
head and bits of me buried in proximity to her stillness,
　even if there is no ghost ship to take me to her neverland,
　I'm going back to that museum
　and I am booking passage
　and I am hoping for the best,
　hoping that she meets me in golden glade or grimy grave as an
angel of anarchy or a festering wretch,
　being whatever it is her will to be and if she gives me leave to
bear witness,
　I will kneel and cry a river when my Violet whispers

"You still don't get it."

And her voice will have made me worth it.

But the sick thing in me that hopes is still alive, and maybe in that darkness that is the shore of light she will see an educated grace in my wretchedness and whisper

"...welcome home..."

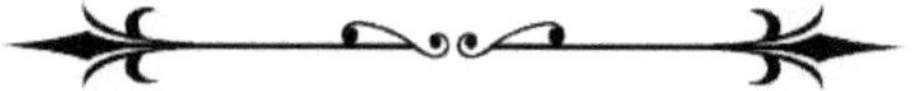

67. The Zymoglyphic Moment

When the raging chaos of the phenomenal world coheres into a kind of poetry…

When dead things use their decay as a door into a different kind of life…

When resonant objects are placed in proximity and reveal the new religion that was hidden by their distance…

When chance slips into your routines to make them holy and synchrosnickety successions of symbols and glyphs and glitches in the mirror lead you to one of those moments, one of THESE moments, maybe…

When the myths that slither under the skin of this gritty simulation expose their malevolent complexity…

When you wander into crooked conversation chambers where the special guests speak sideways…

When the microscope coaxes a cosmos from the microbe…

When the wrong song at the wrong moment, emanating from the wrong window makes an empty street seem to be a missing piece of Hell that is loose in the world, slipping into and out of all the cities. A street that leads to trouble from wherever you are…

When the pills get serious and the melting begins and it's always like you've been here before…

When the lover you spend several lifetimes with in a dream is just an unborn echo in the world you wake up to and every slice of strange you taste makes you remember more of her and the dream and no love you have known in your waking life can compare or compete or complete the procedure that she knew, that she started in you, to free you. A metamorphosis from the many into two. Partly me. Partly you. But with scissors and glue, we collage someone new…

When night is day and dream is awakening…

When it is all obviously an embarrassing abundance of wonders and a million years wouldn't be enough years in which to taste all this….

You have known the Zymoglyphic Moment.

It begins as a taste. It then grows a face. Then it shows you a place. You belong there. And the you you are can't ever get there.

And the you that lives for the seeking doesn't care.

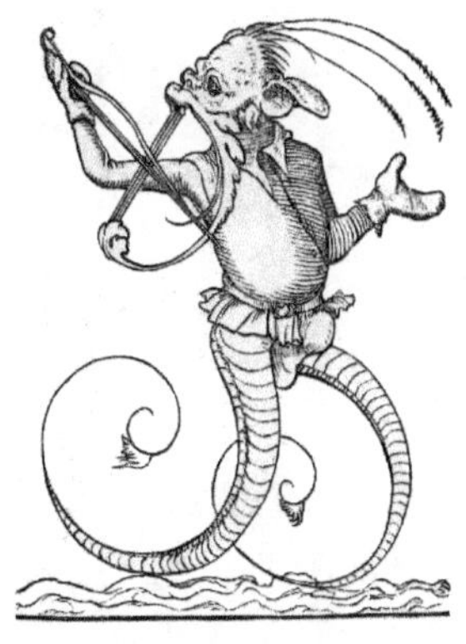

Jason Squamata is a self-described sleazy pulp surrealist and doctor of the psychopompic arts. He is the author of ***Hotel Zymoglyphic,*** an illustrated poem cycle in 66 cantos inspired by an extended visit to the Zymoglyphic region. "The Zymoglyphic Moment" is the newly discovered, never-before published 67th canto of that work. This is the first publication of "Indestructible Object."

Jason is known in Cyberspace as the Orakuloid and more of his work may be seen at orakuloid.blogspot,com

The Perturbation Zone

Leo Daedalus

Prologue

Colonel Svetlana Tereshkova stepped briskly to the podium clutching a bulging file folder in the official blue of the ОКБ-6, to address a crowd that wasn't there. But then, neither was she. She proceeded to debrief those not in attendance about a mission that hadn't occurred, which could be the key to preventing a war that had ended long ago.

Aligning herself with the podium, she noticed that her right bootlace was loose, approaching failure. She was careful to show no sign of that observation. She had learned (or would learn) not to draw attention to topological matters. Her face a battlement of imperturbability, Tereshkova waited for the red light, and then addressed a forest of eccentric baffles arrayed before her to deaden the acoustics of the giant soundstage, empty but for the reproduction of the east half of the briefing room at Scientific-Research Institute N° 38 in which she now stood.

Tereshkova did not open her file folder but delivered a rehearsed précis of its contents calculated for maximum Minkowski plausibility. The folder contained the elements and outline of a speculative fixed-middle chronicle of the events here in question. Per standard practice, retral narrative regression was generated by means of letheogenic memory modification, standard Bayesian hearsay, and the usual arsenal of incompletely corrupted data sources: decayed ledgers, demagnetized tapes, rusty hard drives, etc. Futural narrative extension was effected via a combination of non-linear speculation and classical Humean counterinduction.

Her speech is lost to eternity, as are so many events of that era, thanks to an overzealous application of the principles of historiographic pre-corrosion characteristic of the time. But that is no matter. We offer these details as a matter of interest to those versed in Reidemeister narrative theory. Our lay audience will, we hope, "come along for the ride" and trust that the essential contours of the adventure will become clear enough despite the necessarily convoluted narrative geometry of the account.

Leaving the soundstage, Tereshkova was careful to walk with as natural a gait as possible without tripping on her lace. She

exited the ОКБ-17 and descended the right-hand spiral staircase,
as was her custom. Midway across the plaza she stopped at the
fountain, in the generous shade of a large oak, and put her boot
on a bench. The knot had yet to fail, but it was loose. She exam-
ined it closely. *Damn the child*, she thought to herself with a wry
half-smile. Some weeks ago her young granddaughter Alisa had
informed Tereshkova that she was tying her laces the wrong way.
Most people, the child had explained, use a *babi* knot, named
for all the women who have since time immemorial used it to tie
their headscarves. The correct knot, the straight or reef knot, dif-
fers only, but crucially, in the reversal of one move. Tereshkova
had since mended her ways (the child was right, after all) but the
process of altering a lifetime's muscle memory was a tricky one.
At this stage, she found herself in an uncanny valley in which
both knots, old and new, felt equally unfamiliar. Her self-con-
sciousness sometimes led to overcorrection, as it had this morning. Now her fingers didn't know what to do, and she would have
to reason it out by brute force.

She looked up through the oak leaves at the hot midday sun,
but saw instead a laughing gibbous moon. It was night, and there
was no one about.

[For reasons which will become clear in time, we now Cyrillize the name of
Svetlana Tereshkova, rendering it as "Светлана Терешкова." This standard
Reidemeister move is an expedient narrative maneuver in the event of identity
writhe across alphabet spaces]

Chapter One

Терешкова lightened her step as she passed the open door of the office of her assistant, Secretary-referent Nikolai Ukbaradeh, hoping to put off any new surprises.

"Colonel!" he cheerfully shouted, bounding out of the office.

Терешкова stopped in her tracks, closing her eyes. She didn't know whether to be more irritated or delighted by this irrepressible puppy of a boy fresh from Tajik National University. Терешкова had landed him the job at ОКБ-6 as a favor to a far-flung cousin in Dushanbe.

Nikolai circled around her reading from a glossy American magazine, struggling with his English.

"Legends of space. The brightest star. Colonel Svetlana Tereshkova. Going where no *man*," he paused dramatically, "has gone before."

He held the cover up, beaming. "You are an American superstar!"

Терешкова squinted warily at the glossy, oversaturated cover of *Macrocosm*, from which her unrecognizably retouched face shone, caught in a rare, gleaming smile.

"Ugh," snarled Терешкова. "That American photographer is a practitioner of the dark arts."

"You look like a movie star!"

"As I said."

"Listen," said Nikolai, "I can read you the interview if you like."

"Secretary-referent," sighed Терешкова, "Kolya, thank you. I have a lot to do." She tapped her blue folder meaningfully to sell the lie.

"Okay, yes, of course, Colonel. You take it. When you have time…"

"You keep it, Kolya," said Терешкова as she stepped past him.

"Oh, I have a whole stack. This is for you."

Терешкова stopped and looked wearily at him, amused at her own defeat. "Thank you, Secretary-referent." She took the magazine and he backed away, slightly bowed.

"If you need more!" He put his hands on his chest, bowed his head, and turned.

He has your zadnitsa, *Grishenka,* thought Терешкова to her dead husband, appreciating the fit young man's retreat.

She was careful to leave the magazine on her office table so that Nikolai wouldn't ask about it. But she was equally careful to hide that ridiculous simulacrum of her face under stray papers. She sat at her desk and appreciated its tidiness, a luxurious new development as her work fell off in these last weeks before her retirement. For the first time in years she could see her family photos, revealed now by the erosion of her workpile. The photo of Alisa was very recent, along with the gap in the little girl's front teeth. Терешкова glowered, her face the perfect opposite of her emotional state as she savored the anticipation of becoming a full-time legend not in space exploration but in grandmothering. Grishenka had always teased her that the dourer she looked, the happier it meant she was — unless it simply meant that she was really, truly dour.

The phone rang. Internal line.

"Da."

"Света!" It was Komdiv Vasily Korolev, head of ОКБ-17.

"Vasya," said Терешкова, "did I screw everything up for you?"

"Completely, my dear. We must get out immediately. Finally, will you run away to Antalya with me?"

Терешкова chuckled, "You mangy old wolf."

"One day, one day! Listen, Colonel, I need your expertise."

Терешкова closed her eyes. When Korolev called her "Colonel" the plot invariably thickened.

* * * *

Deep in the sealed subbasement of the ОКБ-17 Quarantine Unit, in the midst of a brightly-lit cube thirty meters on a side, a rail-thin man with a wisp-haired light bulb of a head furrowed his brow with the mortal concentration he had shown as a much younger man defusing bombs in Kulikovo. He was pouring tea, or attempting to, onto a roll of masking tape standing on edge. A handled teacup stood, untouched, at the other end of the table.

Through the one-way mirror, Терешкова grimaced at the poor man's confusion as tea spilled out over the table and poured onto the floor. Korolev studied her reaction.

He guided her by the elbow to the next window. Behind the glass, a large woman in a rumpled navy blue suit sat on the floor in the middle of the room, her legs kicked out in front of her like a panda bear. Every object in the room was arrayed along the circumference of a circle around her at a radius of three meters. She appeared to be reading a book propped up directly in front of her. After a few seconds she crawled over to the book and groped it as if she were blind, looking straight ahead as she turned the page. She crawled back to the center and continued reading.

In the next room a thickly bearded man slept in a precarious sprawl over a heavy rope stretched taut a few centimeters off the floor. A Klein bottle half full of red wine sat on a low table nearby.

"What is wrong with them?" Терешкова asked.

Korolev grunted. "Come."

* * * *

Sealed off in the tranquility of Korolev's elegant, soundproofed office Терешкова looked with bemusement at the bottle of Kentucky bourbon that he held out to her.

"Because you're a big American celebrity now! I thought we could celebrate with this, uh, *boo-ur-bonne*," he said, rolling his R in most un-Kentuckian fashion.

Терешкова sighed. "Fine, fine."

He poured two tumblers and handed her the more generous one.

"I believe they drink it, uh, '*nyet*.'"

"*Neat*," said Терешкова as she saluted him with her raised glass.

They swigged and nodded at each other approvingly.

"They are the survivors from a series of expeditions to Region-Z," explained Korolev.

Терешкова raised an eyebrow.

"There are others," he continued, "but these are the high-functioning ones."

Терешкова took another sip. She was not the type to ask questions before a silence had had the chance to grow thick. Let them play themselves out. Old habit.

Korolev went on. "Dr. Snaut says they suffer from a topological disorder. It affects spatial and in some cases temporal perceptions. Most demonstrate an inability to distinguish among homeomorphs."

Терешкова's eyebrow raised further.

"Or homotopy equivalences?" Korolev tried to remember. "I don't claim to understand the distinction. How's your topology?"

"My topology?" Терешкова laughed. "I don't remember having any."

"There's an old mathematician's joke," said Korolev, "that topologists can't tell the difference between a teacup and a doughnut."

"Ah," said Терешкова, "I remember this. If you had a teacup —"

"With a handle," Korolev interrupted.

"Yes, made of some very flexible material, you could push and pull it into the shape of a doughnut without altering its basic … topological structure."

"Correct."

"So these survivors can't distinguish between a teacup and a doughnut."

"Among other things. There are also temporal effects, and things we don't know how to categorize. They seem to be untethered from the ordinary perceptual structures of space and time. Snaut calls it 'the bends.' He thinks that's funny."

Терешкова smirked. "Have you called Immanuel Kant?"

Korolev returned her smirk. "Uh-huh. He referred us to you, Света."

"So, what, you want me to design a transcendental doughnut?"

"We've been working on this in the shadows, Света. It's … big. And sensitive. And with all the geniuses we have on tap at ОКБ-17, no one has your experience."

Терешкова drew a sharp breath and bit her lower lip. "Dym-kagorod, eh?"

Korolev looked at her apologetically. "It made you stronger. But no, not just that."

"I don't see the connection," grumbled Терешкова, agitated.

"Well," began Korolev, looking down. Терешкова recognized the look of the old soldier marshaling up an argument out of nothing but his own determination.

"You have a feeling," she said.

"Yes, yes," said Korolev, letting go.

Терешкова set her drink down and stood up, putting her hands in her pockets.

"Vasya, I am months — weeks — from retirement. I want to breathe. To make real tea and real doughnuts for my granddaughter. Can't you let an old warhorse go quietly to pasture?"

"I know," Korolev winced. "I don't have to say it's important, right?"

Терешкова sighed like a horse, fluttering her lips.

Korolev, who had been half-sitting on the edge of his desk, bounded over to a small safe on a corner shelf.

"Okay, okay," he said. "You don't have to do anything. Just look at this." He brought her a fifteen millimeter-thick slab of wildly-colored, translucent stone some twenty-five centimeters wide by fifteen centimeters high. It looked like an agate, but the markings had what struck Терешкова as a *deliberateness* to them, as if a volcano had attempted to produce an old-fashioned, ultra-saturated collotype postcard.

"Is this … natural?" She asked.

Korolev shrugged. "Yes?"

She turned it over in her hands, held it up to the light.

"Solonitsyn calls it geophotogenesis," said Korolev. "Speculatively, of course. We call them picture stones."

Терешкова grunted. Korolev could see the hook was set, but lightly. Best now to turn the pressure completely off.

Терешкова brought the stone right up to her nose. "It would be interesting to see it under better light …"

"Take it. Don't worry about it," said Korolev, as casually as he could manage. "Don't let anyone see it," he hastily added.

Терешкова looked at him. "I know what you're doing."

Korolev raised his hands and put on his best innocent face. She gave him her half-smile, eyes probing. The question she really wanted to ask was best set aside for the time being.

* * * *

Nine days later, Komdiv Vasily Korolev walked into the office of Secretary-referent Nikolai Ukbaradeh, giving the young man such a shock that he shot up into a salute, knocking over his chair and sending a cylinder of pens and pencils spilling out across the floor.

"Komdiv!"

"At ease, young man," said Korolev with a chuckle. He got down on his hands and knees to gather up the scattered pens and pencils, just to freak the boy out.

"Oh, sir! No, please, sir! Let me, sir!" stammered Nikolai as he scrambled around the desk. "I mean, unless …" he backpedaled, now terrified that he had somehow countermanded an officer's order.

"Fine, fine, we'll do it together," said Korolev, looking at Nikolai's badge, "Secretary-referent Ukbaradeh."

"Yes, sir."

"Tell me, Secretary-referent, where can I find your boss?"

"Sir, she has been holed up in Laboratory 16 for a week. Sometimes she sends for something, and I bring it to her along with food and drink. Sir."

"Laboratory 16," said Korolev. "Is that the one I just passed with all the, uh … music?"

"Yes, sir. She says she concentrates better with … loud …" Nikolai looked at him helplessly.

"Heavy metal," offered Korolev.

"Yes, sir. Very heavy metal, to be precise," added Nikolai, wincing at his inanity. But Korolev seemed to be interested. Actually, Korolev seemed to be pretty cool.

"Yes. I once bought her a Vällingby record for her birthday.

180-gram vinyl. Smuggled in through Tallinn."

Nikolai gaped.

"So how do I get in there?" Korolev asked. The door was locked, Терешкова had given her "do not disturb" orders, and the metal was louder than an Ilyushin Il-76 at takeoff.

Nikolai considered. "Hypothetically, sir, what would be my liability if you were to gain access to my key? If I had such a key."

"The Colonel might singe your ears off with a few new swear words, but I'll see to it you get some paid time off. Hypothetically."

Nikolai unlocked a desk drawer and handed Korolev a key on a lanyard. Korolev winked at him and turned to go.

"If you want to get on her good side, you'll take that down," he said, pointing at the framed cover of *Macrocosm* magazine hanging opposite Nikolai's desk.

"Sir?"

"It embarrasses her!" Korolev called over his shoulder. "Keep it in your bedroom!"

Nikolai blushed.

Korolev unlocked the door to Laboratory 16 and entered, plugging his ears. Терешкова was hunched over a lab bench running some kind of sensor wand over the picture stone, her goggled face pressed in close. The music was apocalyptic, generating cymatic patterns on all the liquid surfaces in the many bottles, vials, and cylinders in the room. Korolev yelled for her, to no avail. He knew that if he surprised her with a tap on the shoulder he would need medical attention. He switched the lights off and on. She looked up and gave him a big smile. Not what Korolev had expected.

Music off, Терешкова offered him a drink. "Would you like tea? Or a doughnut?"

Korolev laughed, "Whatever you have that's topologically homeomorphic."

To his surprise, she produced both hot tea and stale doughnuts, and bade him sit at the conference table.

"The problem with your boys," said Терешкова, "and they are

all boys at ОКБ-17, aren't they?"

"Ehh, mostly," admitted Korolev.

"— is that they've never been anywhere. They sit inside, in their heads, thinking brilliant rings around the cosmos, but they've never felt the wind on their faces."

Korolev nodded.

Терешкова went on, "Now I'm sure they've told you, Solonitsyn and all the rest, that wherever this Region-Z is," she arched a meaningful eyebrow at him, "there's a perturbation zone — some kind of spatio-temporal interface? — between it and us, no?"

Korolev maintained his poker face. "Go on."

"I think Dr. Snaut is right," said Терешкова. "Those people do have the bends. Not the mundane kind from gross physical decompression but some kind of … I don't know." Korolev gave her her time. She went on gingerly, "I hate, really hate, to say 'metaphysical' decompression, and maybe that's not it really, but I think it is some kind of decompression, for lack of a better term, with respect to our perceptual categories of space and time."

Korolev waited to see if she was finished. She was. "Yes," he said, "'the boys' have said as much, more or less."

They stared at each other, each thinking a riot of thoughts. Korolev reflected that his mind felt louder than the music had a moment ago.

They both spoke at once. Терешкова buttoned her lip and insisted that he speak first.

"Can you get us there?" he asked. "And back?"

She took a deep breath. "You're not going to tell me. You are never going to tell me whether this Region-Z of yours is in fact the mythical Zymoglyphic Region, are you?"

Korolev was a perfect statue. A benevolent one, but marble through and through.

Терешкова nodded. "Then I'll have to find out for myself, won't I?"

Chapter Two

"Welcome to ОКБ-9 Non-Euclidean Travel Test Facility."

Терешкова attempted and failed, most anticlimactically, to push open an unmarked, pocked and weathered door with her shoulder. "Ouch!" she yelped.

"You okay?"

"Dammit," she snarled, rubbing her shoulder. "We're not twenty-two anymore, are we?"

"Speak for yourself," said Korolev.

"Let's try another door."

Korolev looked around at the deserted grounds. They seemed more abandoned junkyard than top-secret, bleeding-edge research facility of yore. "There is no ОКБ-9," he said.

"Right you are," said Терешкова. "There is no ОКБ-9." She pushed open a door and gestured him in. "And yet here we are."

Korolev stepped into an immense hangar populated with the dead or sleeping bodies of strange machines, turbines, cylinders, immense metallic Klein bottles, twisted toroids with cockpits facing opposite directions or turned inside-out, Brancusian wings and eccentric spirals, gears folded in on themselves, mirrored nets, anemones of wiring and conduit, and even a two-headed space helmet. Oil stains mapped the cement floors; chains hung from pipes and beams crisscrossing the ceiling; sheets of glass, mirrors, and multicolored metals stood arrayed in gargantuan shelves, many broken, rusted, crumbling.

"Home, sweet home," said Терешкова, taking it in with a grin, hands on hips.

Korolev whistled.

Терешкова strolled among the machines, her heavy *yuft* boots echoing sepulchrally in the cathedral stillness.

"Did you, uh, fly any of these," asked Korolev, "or whatever they do?"

"Fly, drive, sail, bore, jump — I did it all," remembered Терешкова. "And I was lucky always to miss the ones that killed people."

"Was that …?"

"Very common, yes." She turned to look at Korolev. "It was the norm, really. That's why I have no patience with all the 'hero' nonsense. I was just lucky."

"And talented," said Korolev.

Терешкова harrumphed. She knocked on the side of a machine that looked like an abstract mechanical broccoli some five meters tall, balanced on an improbably narrow foot. It gave a strangely high-pitched ping.

"The woman who tested the proto-prototype of this monstrosity was the best pilot I ever worked with. When the coils fried in orbit, she coaxed it back into the mesosphere against all odds. It blew up after she'd ejected, but a flying hatch took her out. Talent is great, but luck makes the final decision."

Korolev worried that if Терешкова went too far down the cemetery path, mere weeks before her retirement, she'd back out. But he knew better than to argue. "What are we looking for?" he asked.

"That." She pointed to a drab canvas-draped lump in half-darkness fifteen meters away. Korolev was disappointed by its modest and simple form among all these hulking, flanged and betentacled mechanical oddities.

She jogged over to it and yanked the canvas with a flourish. It shredded in her hand, leaving her coughing in a cloud of dust and degraded fibers.

A few minutes later, with the help of a broom and a length of conduit, they had uncloaked the machine. It was an oblong toroid about five meters long and three wide, vaguely egg-shaped from above. From the side it looked like a knobby, overinflated sausage.

"This is the ENELEV-14. We called it the Bedpan."

"Very impressive," said Korolev, in direct opposition to his actual assessment. "Does it work?"

"Once upon a time," said Терешкова, wiping the dust from a porthole, "it very nearly did. Best of all, it never killed me." *Yet.*

"What do we need?" asked Korolev.

"Your best ОКБ-17 boys, and girls, if you have any. Anybody

you trust. Solonitsyn?”

Korolev nodded.

“I’ll bring my team,” said Терешкова, “and something you’re not going to like.”

Korolev gave her a puzzled look.

“Gibarian.”

“*Ёшкин кот!*” exclaimed Korolev, throwing his head back. “That old bastard is long-retired. Isn’t he dead yet?”

“Not yet,” said Терешкова, tickled. “But if it makes you feel better, this could be what does it.”

* * * *

Several weeks later, Терешкова was enjoying a low-key but elegant country dinner at Korolev’s dacha with a few close colleagues. Even Gibarian was there. Also present were Терешкова’s widowed son-in-law, Sergei, and her granddaughter, Alisa. The occasion was what would have been her retirement ceremony. It had been postponed indefinitely, and no one dared mention it.

After dinner, over the Kentucky *boo-ur-bonne* that had become the unofficial official drink of Team Бедпан, Терешкова began, “Now, as much as I hate shoptalk —”

She was met with a barrage of hoots and moans and flung napkins.

“You love nothing more!” cried Gibarian, slapping an irritated Korolev conspiratorially on the shoulder.

“Fine, fine!” admitted Терешкова. “But give an old, still-not-retired-yet warhorse her due.” She leaned in to Alisa, glowering devilishly. “They’ll wish they were rid of me soon enough!” The little girl giggled.

Korolev rang his tumbler with a spoon to silence the room.

Терешкова continued. “You old goats have seen a thing or two, especially you mummified veterans of ОКБ-9,” she pointed her tumbler at Gibarian, who gestured regally in return. “And you young goats, you kids, well, you are about to see how it’s done.”

The room erupted in a drunken cheer. Терешкова silenced them with a raised hand. “Tomorrow.”

"Tomorrow??" shouted Korolev. "Are we — are you — ready?"

"Ready?" Терешкова pointed at him and squinted, her eyelids heavy with drink. "Let's ask my senior advisor." She turned to Alisa and said, "Senior advisor Malenkova, are we ready?"

Alisa giggled again and nodded vigorously, with an emphatic "Da!"

Терешкова turned to Korolev, gloating.

The younger colleagues' eyes darted among the veterans, trying to read the room. The older ones took it all in with detached amusement.

Korolev gave his old nemesis, Gibarian, an imploring look.

Gibarian shrugged. "We've tested, and tested, and tested three times again. And I know you'd be happy about it, but if we test one more time, it might just kill me."

Korolev looked at Терешкова. She was the picture of a perfect hangover. "Monday," he said.

Терешкова nodded and waved her assent, as if to say, "Yes, Monday. That's what I meant."

Natalya Makarova, the gifted young cartographer, let out a big, involuntary sigh of relief, prompting laughter all around. The laughter nonetheless belied the worry troubling everyone in the room, except Alisa.

* * * *

Very early Monday morning, in the darkness approaching low tide, Team Bedpan assembled in the makeshift mess, some groggy, some wide-eyed with adrenaline. They drank strong, hot tea from a Klein samovar constructed as a gag by one of the machinists, a goofy Lithuanian named Banionis. And, of course, they ate doughnuts. No one spoke. Everyone knew their job.

Soon after dawn, Korolev appeared. They had duly informed him that embarkation would be just after high tide, at about noon, and that there wouldn't be much to see before then. But he was a man of experience, and he knew better than most how to see things.

The caisson pumps were thrumming away. Agitators sent up

plumes of salt mist and sea smells. The Bedpan, now reborn as the ENELEV-15, hung at head level like a caught jellyfish, suspended over the trap doors of the launch canal. Korolev was dismayed to see that it looked, if anything, in worse shape than when he and Терешкова had unveiled it that afternoon weeks before. It was now pitted and streaked with rust, its copper surfaces bruised with verdigris, and encrusted with living barnacles and limpets. It looked like a sorry salvage that might have been more mercifully left on the ocean floor. Korolev said as much.

Терешкова chuckled. "Sometimes the right kind of wrong is better than the wrong kind of right."

"What's that supposed to mean?" asked Korolev.

Терешкова sipped her tea. "We pored over your expedition reports with a fine-toothed … well, an electron microscope."

Gibarian interrupted from atop the Bedpan, where he was taking some kind of reading, "They were so heavily redacted, Vasya, you could have saved money on ink by just sending us blank paper!"

"He has a point," grumbled Терешкова, "but we scoured them with the eyes not of your soft-handed theoreticians but of weather-bitten explorers, eh?" She flexed a bicep at him.

"And?"

"Your pencil boys want everything shiny and idealized: perfect lines, perfect Bézier surfaces, perfect materials in perfect polish. And sure, sometimes that's exactly what you need. Especially when you're fishing for funding, right?" She rubbed her thumb and fingers together at Korolev, who blinked indulgently. "But this isn't an airshow. Non-Euclidean travel is …" she waggled her hand. "It's a weird business."

"So — rust?" Korolev said, tapping a thick patch of it with a tentative digit.

"Decay!" Терешкова exulted. "The bite marks of time itself! The fundamental intrusion of time on matter, on form, on space. It's the proof that we've been *through* it, through time. It is the shape the past takes in the present. And this Region-Z of yours … to get us through the Perturbation Zone … bidirectionally, mind you ….” She was struggling.

Gibarian pitched in from above, “‘Non-Euclidean’ is an inadequate term, Vasya, a legacy from a simpler day. The Perturbation Zone is not so much a spatio-temporal interface — a frontier, or membrane — as it is a transformation. It’s not a border you cross into, and then cross back out of. It changes you, and if you don’t change again — anew — on the way home, in just the right way … well, you’ve seen what happens.”

Korolev looked at them both watching him expectantly. “I don’t understand. In the least.”

“We’re on the hunt,” Терешкова tried to clarify, “for a continuous function between topological spaces that comes with a continuous *inverse* function.”

“But there may not be an inverse function!” Gibarian cautioned. “In which case …”

“In which case what??” demanded Korolev.

Терешкова drew a finger across her throat and stuck out her tongue.

“No, no, no!” cried Gibarian. “This is why, for heaven’s sake, we have the perturbation theory!” Seeing Korolev’s blank, slightly horrified look, Gibarian elaborated. “It’s simple. We take a problem we know how to solve completely, a simpler problem that approximates our real problem.”

“Like … what?” Korolev asked. “Like the bends? Ordinary decompression?”

“Sure, sure,” said Gibarian impatiently. “Then we bring in successive complicating factors — tractable ones — iteratively *perturbing* our initial model and then correcting for those perturbations, nudging it all toward an ever-closer approximation of the conditions we will meet on the ground. Within a calculable deviation. No?”

“So …” Korolev struggled to squeeze out any sense he could. “The rust? The barnacles? Are perturbations?”

“Yyy-yes,” Gibarian granted, “you could say that.”

Korolev rubbed his eyes. “This is making my head hurt.”

Gibarian laughed, “You’re in good company! Newton himself,

the great Sir Isaac, when he was working on the Moon's orbit, said," Gibarian switched to English, "'*It causeth my head to ache.*'"

"*Causeth*?" said Korolev, his utilitarian English failing him.

"Old-fashioned English," explained Gibarian, translating: "'It gives me a headache.'"

Korolev shook his head at them. "Honestly, is all this just your expensive jargon for 'guesswork?'"

Терешкова and Gibarian laughed.

"Just tell me one thing," Korolev looked up at Gibarian. "Will she come back? The same?"

Gibarian shrugged elaborately.

"Yes, Vasya," said Терешкова. "You know I wouldn't go if I believed otherwise. Not now."

* * * *

At 12:04 Терешкова was suited up and ready to go. The final medical and psych tests had gone without a hitch. Natalya Makarova had brought her a packet of up-to-the-minute maps and charts. She had pressed a three-leaf clover into one of the salinity maps.

"Isn't it supposed to have four leaves for luck?" asked Терешкова, gently teasing her.

The young woman was earnest. "My *babka* said it's a poor kind of luck that you can't rely on finding when you need it. Three-leaf clovers are luck you can always depend on."

Protocol specified that Junior lieutenant Dvorzhetsky should assist Терешкова into the vessel and seal the cockpit, but Korolev insisted on doing the honors. As Терешкова got into position, prone in the portside bay of the toroid, Korolev had to ask, "Why is there a second cockpit, facing rearward?"

"That?" replied Терешкова, "That's for the return trip."

Korolev's lips began to form the obvious question, but he thought better of it. Instead he tightened a strap and asked, "All set?"

"Affirmative, Komdiv," said Терешкова.

"I brought you something," he said, holding it awkwardly over her head where she could reach it.

"Vällingby?!" exclaimed Терешкова.

"I trust you installed a recklessly loud sound system in this bucket, yes?"

"Thank you, Vasilyushka," said Терешкова. "I will see you …"

"When I see you," said Korolev. He closed the hatch.

Chapter Three

"Boredom."

"Boredom?" echoed the journalist.

Терешкова tried out a variety of modifiers. "Stultifying boredom. Abject boredom. Coma-inducing boredom." She settled on "categorical boredom."

"Categorical … boredom," repeated the journalist, jotting it down in his notebook. "Why did you launch from Komkenanka, so far away, instead of airlifting the ENELEV-15 to a position nearer the vicinity of Region-Z? Wouldn't that have saved you an immense amount of pointless travel?"

"Pointless." Терешкова turned the word around in her head. "We thought …. We calculated …. We *felt* that it was critical to maintain the integrity of the journey, the whole journey. Our hypothesis …. We came to believe that part of the problem that had afflicted the previous expeditions was a gap in meaning. Accordingly, we saw fit to calculate a logotropic trajectory. It was necessary that Point A be properly motivated. To cheat the curve and deposit the Bedpan — ENELEV-15 — *in media res*, as it were, would jeopardize the mission."

"You had to start at the beginning," said the journalist.

"Correct."

"Ironic, isn't it?" said the journalist. "Your official departmental chronicles all launch *in media res*, do they not? Reidemeister narrative theory, Minkowski plausibility conics, all that. There are those who would suggest that the Institute runs entirely on obfuscation."

Терешкова considered this. The notebook yawned.

"Was that the first time you died, or …?" the journalist paused, tapping his pen against his cheek.

The notebook grasped him in its talons and flew off, screeching.

Терешкова shook herself. She had not been asleep, not dreaming, but her daydreams had been growing ever more fantastic in proportion to the relentless, accumulating sameness of the journey.

At one point she had the distinct feeling that she had been there before, and worried that she might have made a circle. But her course checked out and triple-checked out. She looked out the porthole at the same featureless sky above and featureless sea below and wondered how she could even have formed the idea of having previously been anywhere in particular in this undifferentiated vastness. It gave her a shiver.

One day, the radio crackled. She thought she heard the decayed germ of a voice. It seemed a familiar voice, if it was anything.

Two days later she heard it again, a little clearer and a little more persistent.

"Allo?" she said.

The voice faded and swelled, curling around the interior of the craft.

"Allo?"

"Allo?" the voice replied.

"Who is this?"

"You must pull back!" said the voice.

"Pull back?"

The voice crumbled away.

"Allo?"

"Lieutenant, get out! Now, Светочка!"

Светочка? Lieutenant?

"Stepan?" Терешкова asked, shaking. "Styopochka, is that you?"

"Who do you think it is, Genghis Khan??"

Dymkagorod came flooding back. The wrecked convoy, the smell of ordnance, the clunky old radio. She felt its heft. Her eyes watered, not from emotion but from the smoke.

"Styopochka, this — thirty years have passed."

"Just get the hell out of there!"

"What … what if I don't?"

"What?? Don't be crazy!"

"What if I can get to you? It's not far. Maybe this time …"

"We are secure, Lieutenant! Your position is not. Get out, now!"

"Styopochka …"

And then came the blast, exactly as she had tried to forget it for three decades. She did nothing but shake, in that crazy vessel, in the middle of the ocean, for what felt like hours.

When she awoke the next morning, she checked the ship's recorder. It faithfully played back a recording of the conversation she had had with a man thirty years dead, thousands of kilometers away. No matter how many times she listened, expecting it to vanish like a dream, there it was, cold as stone. She was approaching the Perturbation Zone, right on schedule.

"Let's get started." The journalist was back. Only this time the daydream was more vivid. She felt the couch beneath her, smelled the sweet tobacco smoke from his pipe. He was now, in fact, more psychoanalyst than reporter. And the notebook was no longer a bird of prey but a blue-gray cat licking its paws, having a bath.

"Tell me about Stepan," the journalist prompted.

"Ugh," Терешкова sighed. "It's such a cliché."

"A cliché?"

"Yes. The whole mythology of the 'defining moment.'"

"Was it not a defining moment?"

"It was an entire career ago! Thirty years!"

"Thirty- …" the analyst consulted his notes, "… five, yes?"

"Thirty, thirty-five," said Терешкова. "What difference does it make?"

"You are familiar with Freud's topographic theory of the mind?"

"Um … the superego and all that?"

"Earlier, earlier," said the analyst, "in *The Interpretation of Dreams*. The iceberg as a model of the three levels of the mind. In this model the conscious is the exposed tip of the iceberg. It is all the mental activity you are aware of. Just below the surface is the preconscious. You are not actively aware of its contents, but they are easily retrievable from memory. Like the proper method for tying a bootlace, hmm? But the bulk of the iceberg is hidden in the sunless depths, inaccessible: the unconscious. This is where resides all you do not want to see."

What am I doing here? wondered Терешкова.

"Selfish and immoral urges, violent impulses, inadmissible sexual desires. Traumatic experiences. Shame. Dymkagorod, no?"

"What?"

"Did you love him?"

"Stepan? Of course."

"You desired him."

"What? No! He was my brother!"

"Your brother! In the same regiment?"

Терешкова sighed. "We grew up together. He was not technically my brother, by blood or by law, but yes, in every meaningful way."

"Mm-hmm."

"What?"

"Well. It's easy to understand that all this ambiguity in your relationship with Stepan would precipitate sharp ambivalence, the tensions of which would cause deep unconscious perturbation. It's only natural that you would want him to die."

"What??"

"That being unacceptable, of course, you would naturally create a story in which you had no choice, in which, indeed, Stepan himself would order you to abandon him. You left him to die, correct?"

Терешкова started to laugh.

"Ah! Laughter," said the analyst. "A typical reaction."

Терешкова was fairly shaking with laughter. "I'm being bullied by my own hallucination! A hackneyed cliché in pince-nez! Thousands of kilometers to sea, without an iceberg in sight!"

"Very interesting," said the analyst, though he was beginning to melt. The cat looked up with only mild interest.

And then, as Colonel Терешкова later told it, "things got weird."

* * * *

A thorough analysis of all available data — including but not limited to ship's recordings, instrument readings, official logs and personal journals, direct testimony and hearsay, dream reports, meteorological data, metallurgical data, divination, entheogenic interventions, hypnopolygraphy, and heuristical neuroreconnaissance, all rigorously cross-factored and Reidemeister-normalized — definitively precludes all possibility of describing or in any way communicating, tabulating, representing, or metaphorizing either the measurable events or the phenomenology of Colonel Терешкова's crossing through the Perturbation Zone. (We direct the extravagantly persistent reader to the hermeneutical-poetic account attempted by Orbeliani et al. in A Totemic Perturbation Series in Sympathy with ENELEV-15, *though we disavow any liability in connection with same.)*

The sole intelligible datum to be extracted from Colonel Терешкова's personal account of the crossing is her clear and distinct recollection of having said, in English, at a moment of peak intensity, "It causeth my head to ache."

* * * *

Терешкова awoke on a beach of coarse, lurid sand. The air was thick, humid, viscoelastic and sweet like the heady lotus-nectar of the genus *Nepenthes*. The sky was of a blue that struck her as too blue, *too much like the sky*. She felt the beach shifting under her. She sprang to her feet. Hundreds, thousands of craggy shellfish scuttled in the sand, roughly following after the ebb tide. A gleam to the right — the east? — caught her eye. It was the Bedpan, far downshore, beached high and dry and, apparently, intact. That was a good sign.

Терешкова turned to face the island and started. She was face-to-face, or pupil-to-pupil, with the serpentine stalk of a scaly plant tipped with an eyeball that regarded her with curiosity. "Hoh!" she exclaimed. "Well. This is absolutely, definitely, beyond a doubt the Zymoglyphic Region."

The eyeball plant made no reply.

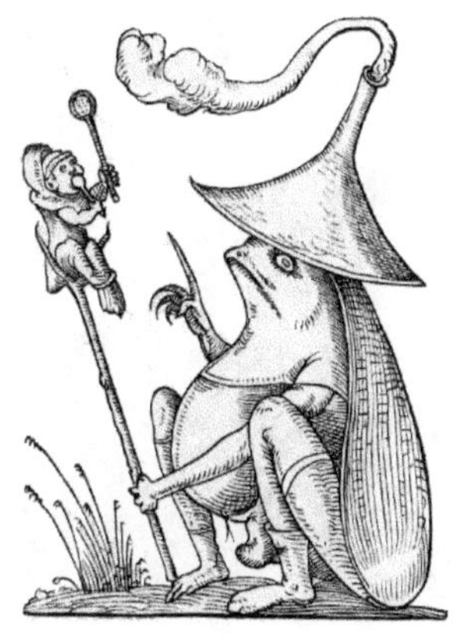

Leo Daedalus is a multitalented performer and writer best known as the producer and impresario for Portland's semi-underground avant-variety-talkshow *The Late Now* (2012-2016). He has recently relocated to Los Angeles to pursue a career in stand-up comedy.

The Perturbation Zone is a forthcoming novella, of which the first three chapters are presented here. More to come!

$1

Literary Guest Book

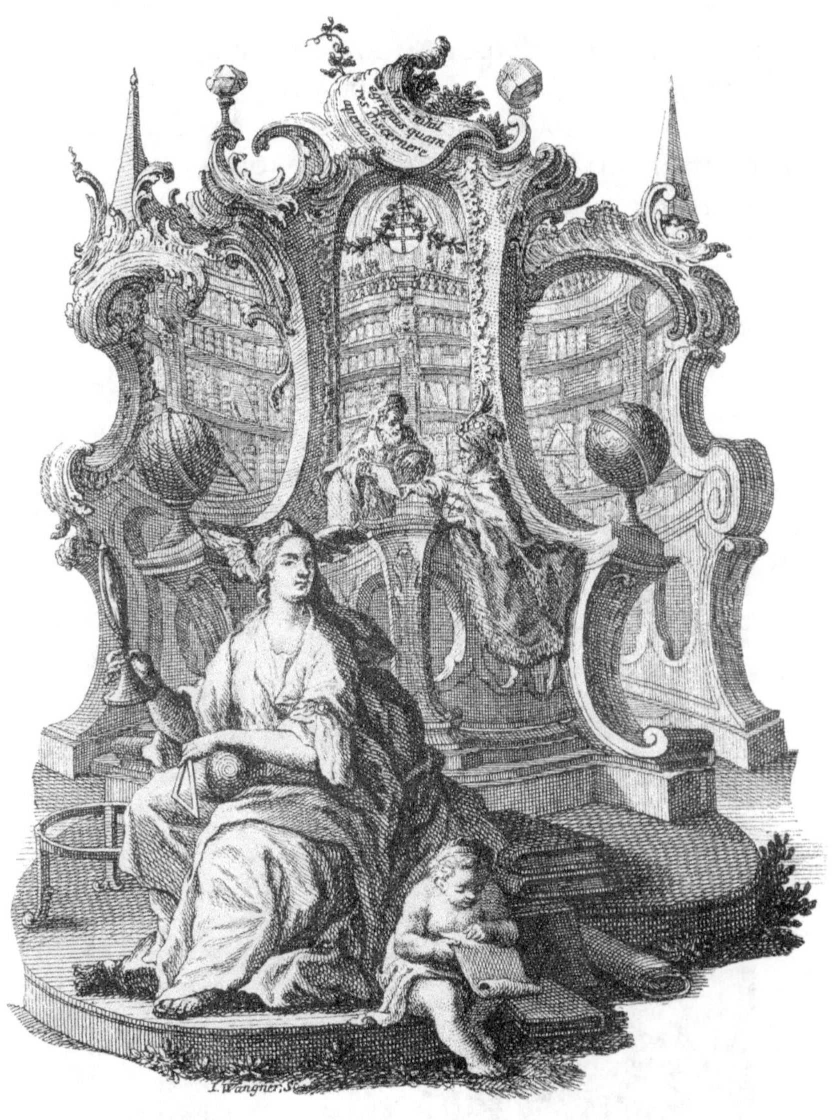

The Zymoglyphic Museum

THE ZYMOGLYPHIC MUSEUM HAS EXISTED, AT
LEAST IN SPIRIT, FOR CENTURIES. IT HAS BEEN
FORTUNATE TO HAVE BEEN VISITED BY SEVERAL
IMPORTANT LITERARY FIGURES, ALTHOUGH
THEY HAVE COME AWAY WITH VERY DIFFERENT
IMPRESSIONS.

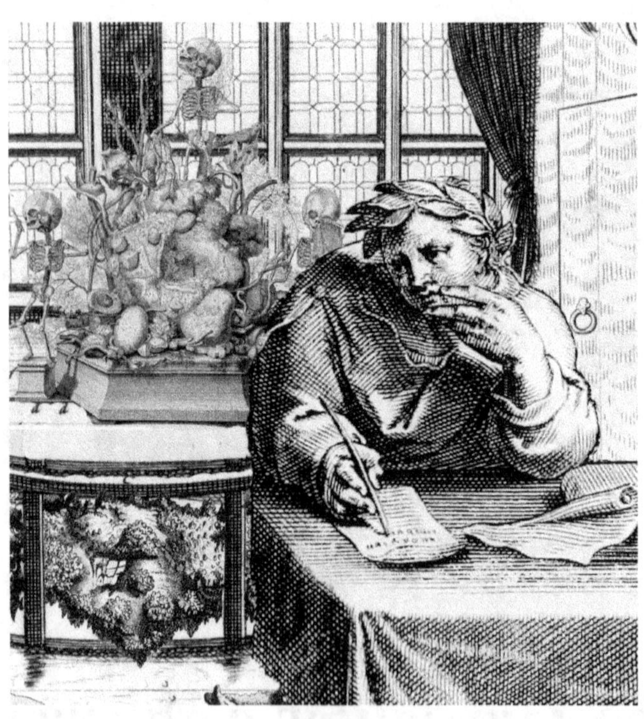

"...a goodly huge Cabinet, wherein whatsoever the Hand of Man
by Art or Engine has made rare in Stuff, Form or Motion; whatsoever Singularity, Chance, and the Shuffle of things hath produced,
whatsoever Nature has wrought in things that want Life and may
be kept, shall be sorted and included"

-- Sir Francis Bacon, *Gesta Grayorum*, 1594

Finds tongues in trees, books in the running brooks,
Sermons in stones and good in every thing.

-- Wm. Shakespeare, "As You Like It", 1599

...a tortoise hung,
An alligator stuff'd, and other skins
Of ill-shaped fishes...
A living drollery.

-- Wm. Shakespeare, "The Tempest", 1610

"[E]very man to his own taste...Have not the wisest of men in
all ages, not excepting Solomon himself,—have they not had
their Hobby-Horses;—their running horses,—their coins and
their cockle-shells, their drums and their trumpets, their fiddles,
their pallets,—their maggots and their butterflies?—and so long
as a man rides his Hobby-Horse peaceably and quietly along the
King's highway, and neither compels you or me to get up behind
him,—pray, Sir, what have either you or I to do with it?"

-- Laurence Sterne, *Tristram Shandy*, 1759

"affords more pabulum to the brain than all the Frusts and Crusts
and Rusts of antiquity which travelers can cook up for it"

-- Laurence Sterne, *A Sentimental Journey*, 1765

Spider claw and hoptoad paunch
And winglets to the gnome!
No true beastie will you launch
Albeit a little poem...
You all can feel the secret virtue
Of Nature constantly at work,
As rising effluents alert you
To powers that deep within her lurk

-- Johann Goethe, Faust (tr. W. Arndt) 1808

"a considerable miscellany of things and shadows of things: History in authentic fragments lay mingled with Fabulous chimeras, wherein also was reality; and the whole not as dead stuff, but as living pabulum, tolerably nutritive for a mind as yet so peptic"

"What is all this but a mad Fermentation; wherefrom, the fiercer it is, clearer product will one day evolve itself?"

-- Thomas Carlyle, Sartor Resartus, 1834

"expressive of a mind which has reached the gelatinous mildewy stage in the mortification of all healthy and courageous thought"

-- H.D. Thoreau, Walden, 1847

"all this mixes with your most mystic mood; so that fact and fancy, halfway meeting, interpenetrate, and form one seamless whole"

-- Herman Melville, Moby-Dick, 1851

"The management of this institution has had a severe though not painful attack of novelty on the brain...It is well worth a visit... There are many other things here which make one lift his eyes and wonder at the freaks of Nature when she is in a frolicsome mood."

-- Mark Twain, 1864
(from a review of Gilbert's Museum in the San Francisco Daily
Morning Call)

After all not to create only, or found only,
But to bring perhaps from afar what is already founded,
To give it our own identity, average, limitless, free...
In large calm halls, a stately Museum shall teach you the infinite,
solemn lessons of Minerals

> -- Walt Whitman, "Song of the Exposition", 1871

"imaginary gardens with real toads in them"

> -- Marianne Moore, "Poetry", 1924

"a conglomeration at any rate of the most heterogeneous and
ill-assorted objects, piled higgledy-piggledy...proved that when
the shrivelled skin of the ordinary is stuffed out with meaning it
satisfies the senses amazingly."

> -- Virginia Woolf, *Orlando*, 1928

"...beneath the flowers, down the dark avenues into the unlit
world where the leaf rots and the flower has fallen...Down there
among the roots where the flowers decayed, gusts of dead smells
were wafted; drops formed on the bloated sides of swollen things.
The skin of rotten fruit broke, and matter oozed too thick to run.
Yellow excretions were exuded by slugs, and now and again an
amorphous body with a head at either end swayed slowly from
side to side."

> -- Virginia Woolf, *The Waves*, 1931

"...lumpish hybrid things which only fantasy could spawn....
gorgons, chimaeras, dragons, cyclops, and all their shuddersome
congeners...hideous parodies on forms of organic life we know...
an evil-looking crypt lighted dimly by dusty windows...isolated
parts of problematical entities whose assembled forms were the
phantoms of delirium."

> -- H.P. Lovecraft, "The Horror at the Museum", 1932

"Penetrators are permitted into the museomound free...This is the
way to the museyroom. Mind your hats goan in!...you would see
in his house of thoughtsam...what a jetsam litterage of convolvuli
of time lost or strayed, of lands derelict and of tongues laggin,
too...the crux of the catalogue of our antediluvial zoo...A middenhide hoard of objects!...Mind your boots goan out. Phew!"

-- James Joyce, *Finnegans Wake*, 1939

"...everything oozes..."

-- Samuel Beckett, "Waiting for Godot", 1949

"where the faculties of the skull no longer admit the worms of
the senses"

-- Allen Ginsberg, "Howl", 1956

"...a museum of mortal remains - of endoskeletons and exoskeletons - of shells, coral, bone, cartilage, and chitin - of dottles and
orts and residua of souls long gone."

-- Kurt Vonnegut, *The Sirens of Titan*, 1959

"What's this museum up here?—"Let's go in and find out"—
That's the way Ben is, he doesn't know what's going on either
but at least he waits to find out maybe—But the museum is
closed—We stand there on the steps looking at the closed door—
"Hey," I say, "the temple is closed"

-- Jack Kerouac, *Big Sur,* 1960

"It seems to be some very extensive museum, a place of many
levels, and new wings that generate like living tissue - though
if it all does grow toward some end shape, those who are here
inside can't see it."

-- Thomas Pynchon, *Gravity's Rainbow*, 1973

"formal rot to be enjoyed on a theoretical level...soft with dust and shadow, everywhere the ruck of clustered objects, most of them plainly put together and left to themselves to grow into the look of familiar things"

-- Don DeLillo, *Ratner's Star,* 1976

"We walk the familiar and always changing halls now in amusement, now in skepticism, now seeing little but cleverness in the whole questionable enterprise, now struck with enchantment...We may doubt the museum, but we do not doubt our need to return. For we are restless, already we are impatient to move through the beckoning doorways, which lead to rooms with other doorways that give dark glimpses of distant rooms, distant doorways, unimaginable discoveries. And is it possible that the secret of the museum lies precisely here, in its knowledge that we can never be satisfied?...for us it's enough, for us it is almost enough."

-- Steven Millhauser, "The Barnum Museum", 1987

"As supernatural as a Visitant from the Regime of Death to the sunny Colony of Life, -- to be metaphorickal about it"

-- Thomas Pynchon, *Mason & Dixon,* 1997

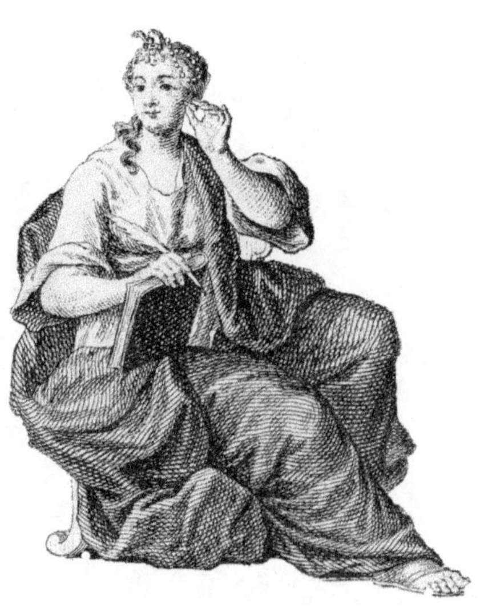

End Notes

Credits

Cover design by Gigi Little (gigilittle.com)

Cover art by Jim Stewart based on eco-dye print by Judith Hoffman and engravings from Ernst Haeckel's *Die Radiolarien* (1862, reprinted by Prestel Verlag as *Art Forms from the Ocean*, 2005)

Author bio illustrations from *The Drolatic Dreams of Pantagruel* (1565) via Public Domain Review (original artist uncredited)

Ornate dividers in "Indestructible Object" from Freepik.com

More from the Zymoglyphic Museum Press

Hotel Zymoglyphic by Jason Squamata

The Zymoglyphic Museum: A Guide to the Collections

Views of the Zymoglyphic Region

Sketches of the Zymoglyphic Region

...as well as various booklets, some of which are included in this compilation.

See zymoglyphic.org/pubs.html for details

www.ingramcontent.com/pod-product-compliance
Lightning Source LLC
Chambersburg PA
CBHW052354060726
47592CB00020B/2244